Professional Practice in Architecture

FRANK ORR

Professional Practice in Architecture

VNR VAN NOSTRAND REINHOLD COMPANY
NEW YORK   CINCINNATI   TORONTO   LONDON   MELBOURNE

Copyright © 1982 by Van Nostrand Reinhold Company
Library of Congress Catalog Card Number 81-19692
ISBN 0-442-27065-8 (cloth)
ISBN 0-442-26391-0 (paper)

Printed in the United States of America.
Designed by Rose Delia Vasquez

Published by Van Nostrand Reinhold Company
135 West 50th Street
New York, NY 10020

Van Nostrand Reinhold Limited
1410 Birchmount Road
Scarborough, Ontario M1P 2E7, Canada

Van Nostrand Reinhold Australia Pty. Ltd.
17 Queen Street
Mitcham, Victoria 3132, Australia

Van Nostrand Reinhold Company Limited
Molly Millars Lane
Wokingham, Berkshire, England

16 15 14 13 12 11 10 9 8 7 6 5 4 3 2 1

Library of Congress Cataloging in Publication Data

Orr, Frank, 1932–
    Professional practice in architecture.

    Bibliography: p.
    Includes index.
    1. Architectural practice—United States.
I. Title.
NA1996.O77   720'.68   81-19692
ISBN 0-442-27065-8   AACR2
ISBN 0-442-26391-0 (pbk.)

CONTENTS

ACKNOWLEDGMENTS   vii

INTRODUCTION   viii

Part I The Working Environment
of the Architect   1

1 The American Construction Economy   3

2 Elements in the Construction Process   8

3 The Consumers   12

4 The Design Professionals   17

5 The Constructors   22

6 Consultants, Specialists, and Other Participants   28

7 Governmental Authorities   34

8 Codes, Ordinances, and Other Legal Considerations   41

Part II Professional Organization,
Management, and Procedure   45

 9 The Professional Design Office   47
10 Office Organizational Patterns   54
11 Internal Office Management   64
12 Financial Management   71
13 Office Management by Project   80
14 The Project Processes   86
15 Other Services   112
16 Future Trends   117
17 Summary and Recapitulation   123

APPENDIX 1 Bibliography   126
APPENDIX 2 Typical Forms   128
INDEX   145

Acknowledgments

There are many to whom thanks are due for helping with this effort. Prominent are:

John Mitchell, for encouraging me to try;

The late Edwin Keeble, my former employer and mentor of many years, from whom much of the content originally came;

Wendy Lochner, my wise and kind editor;

Ed Houk, my partner, for not only putting up with the time loss and other distractions the effort generated, but also for sharing his wisdom in architectural matters;

Nancy, who continues to be supportive and loving even though playing one of life's most difficult roles, the wife of an architect.

INTRODUCTION

The overriding, guiding purpose of erecting a building is to get from here to there—namely, from the perceived need to the realized, completed, and occupied building.

Despite some appearances, the purpose is not to produce fine, exacting, and beautiful drawings, nor complete and concise specifications, as helpful as these may be in realizing the real goal. These are only means, subordinate to the end product—either, in short term, a single building or, in the long view, a consistently high-quality output of many buildings over the duration of a professional practice. (The latter of these goals may even be said to be subordinate to the former, since the user/consumer "buys" only a single project, whether one or a number of buildings, not a lifetime practice.)

Both the Roman architect Vitruvius and the Italian Renaissance architect Alberti gave us three "ways" of architecture—utility, strength, and beauty (or firmness, commodity, and delight). In the daily activities of a person involved as a small cog in the building-production machine, it may be easy to become fixed on the utility or strength of architecture and to overlook its beauty or delight.

Architects must always focus on the real, fundamental, rock-bottom objectives of their activity, no matter how small or large, narrow or wide their contribution may seem to be. In my opinion, the practice of architecture has two such basic objectives, both stated or implied above—to produce buildings that satisfy human needs and to evaluate one's work constantly, to measure it against the principles of ''firmness, commodity, and delight.''

It is not enough to provide structures that will remain standing under all loading conditions, roofs that will not leak, and environmental systems that maintain human bodily comfort. While the majority of the design and delivery team may not participate in a direct way in the decisions affecting the ''delight'' aspects, their sympathy to these choices or lack thereof can profoundly affect the success of a building in meeting the visual criteria.

A building has been defined as a structure that separates inside spaces from the outside environment for the primary purpose of creating comfortable conditions for the occupant. As we have noted above, expanding this definition to include the aspects of beauty transforms it into a definition of architecture. Architectural practice, therefore, might be said to be the organization of the labor necessary to produce architecture. Unfortunately, this definition is somewhat too broad in that at least over the last one hundred years or so, for most projects the architect is just one of a triumvirate necessary to produce architecture.

The opening chapters of this book explore these elements as well as others that play ancillary roles in the decision-design-delivery process. In order to understand the role of the ''design'' member of this trio, it is necessary to understand, in a comprehensive way, the entirety of the process and its participants.

Later chapters examine the general internal and external elements and organization of professional architectural practice. According to a recent AIA survey approximately 80 percent of America's registered architects work in offices of ten people or less and prefer to do so. The discussions in this book focus on the types of activities likely to be encountered in offices of this size. However, where appropriate, mention is made of the alternatives available to larger or smaller offices.

The last part of the book looks into the future, identifying trends that may develop into standard practices and patterns.

What this book does not do is attempt to teach design, presentation, marketing, energy analysis, or any similar specialized activity. It does attempt to show how to organize a professional office as well as one's own assignments in order to perform these tasks more effectively.

Part I

THE WORKING ENVIRONMENT OF THE ARCHITECT

1

The American Construction Economy

Everyone, even people living in the most tightly controlled socialist societies, engages in business with some frequency. Every time you purchase or sell anything, you enter into a business contract, even if it involves only a loaf of bread.

In the United States, as in most of the western world, freely entered business contracts are the norm and almost all exchanges of goods and services occur in this manner. This means that the laws of supply and demand are very much in action and have a great effect on what is produced for sale and what is purchased, even when government seeks through regulation to moderate the extremes.

These same laws or forces affect the construction industry as much as or perhaps more than most other segments of our economy. It is, by and large, a free economy, meaning that individuals or freely associated groups perceive the need for and initiate the process of constructing a building. The relationships and interactions among parties involved in this process are complex and varied but function, in the main, in a free-enterprise atmosphere, one paying another for value received.

Construction involves many skills, tools, and types of entrepreneurs and government regulators and provides employment for a large number of people. The greatest numbers are found in the

3

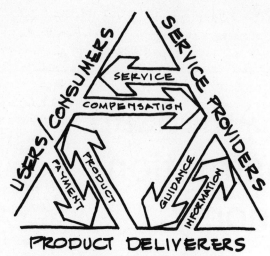

1-1   The Way the Economy Works

physical construction of a building, the last phase in the sequence. The entire industry as well as a typical individual building project might be described as an inverted pyramid, with the number of people increasing as the project progresses. One conclusion is that, if high employment is a public goal, then that goal is best served if as many projects as possible progress from the planning stage into actual construction.

Unfortunately, and almost always due to circumstances beyond control, much of what architectural offices begin to work on does not eventually result in actual construction. The primary reason for this is that the financial feasibility of many projects cannot be determined without preliminary design study and evaluation. Upon investigation, it may be found that some of these projects are simply not feasible, at least within the resources of those proposing them. Thus, some will eventually become ''real'' projects, but many will not.

Another prominent reason is that the workload for many, primarily smaller, architectural offices fluctuates widely, and occasionally nonconstruction commissions are undertaken to supplement income. Depending on local needs and the firm's connections, these may include projects in such areas as graphic design, site evaluation, and interior design, although the last may rightfully be considered an integral part of architectural practice.

In a free economy, construction expresses the public will in a direct way, though moderated by a lag due to its huge costs and extended time requirements. The public gets what it desires enough to pay for. Much that is built is initiated and sponsored by government, but even here market forces are at work, since the industry responding to its initiative is overwhelmingly in private hands.

The public goals that are addressed and hopefully met in what architects build are generally an expression of the social values of the time. For example, the interstate-highway system was planned when the automobile was considered to be the best possible means of personal transportation and its use likely to continue to grow indefinitely. However, according to law all construction must also satisfy the goals of health, safety, and welfare. Society, through government and voluntary covenants, has established standards to ensure a minimum level of conformity with these goals, although these can shift with changing social policies.

Under the blanket term "public welfare" a great many subgoals may be found: accessibility for the handicapped; the ability to prevent constructions or practices that may not be unhealthy or unsafe but are nuisances or unsightly; the preservation of historical buildings that contribute to the character and meaning of a locale; and, in a few cases, the ability to prescribe strict design constraints. But, perhaps a better definition of public welfare would be: that which enriches and ennobles mankind, that which calls forth the best in us, which encourages us to act most responsibly in our use of limited resources and in our relations with each other—in short, those traits that should be found in buildings if good architecture has been produced.

In all the diverse activities of a construction project, the people engaged must be paid and their expenses met or their part of the work will not be done and the project will not proceed. This means that sufficient money has to be invested in the project at each level to cover the costs. Too often developers or would-be developers attempt to promote a project without understanding this very basic principle or without recognizing that it applies to them, and they expect other parties to work for unreasonably low or sometimes even no income. Since architects are among the first actors to appear in the scenario, they are often asked to contribute preliminary services "just to help get the project off the ground" or at least to accept an income lower than office expenses require. This is not good practice for an architect in particular nor for the public in general.

The American economy functions, as we have observed, on the basis of freely entered business agreements. Money for this activity must be found, and it is found by, controlled by, and flows from the sponsor or sponsors of the project. The "sponsors" may not be the original initiators but are always the parties who propel the project into the construction phase. If they do not have ready funds, they must either borrow them or find other parties who will invest in the project, holding an equity in it and its income-producing ability after completion.

When money is available, the project can proceed and those involved will be assured of receiving their due remuneration for their labors, services, or products. The precise cash flow can be rather complex and usually increases in complexity in direct proportion to the size of the project. Some payments are made directly by the sponsor, or "owner," as is the more common identification, and others are made indirectly through other parties, including the architect. At any rate, the owner ultimately makes all payments, and the architect and other participants are therefore obligated to satisfy their contractual arrangements and to meet the owner's specifications, as long as they are consistent with legal and ethical requirements.

Without such relationship and commitment the process, at least in the long term, would not function. Likewise, all the participants under contract must trust one another. This includes those outside direct-pay relationships, such as the governmental officials who administer the codes and other regulations under which construction is allowed. Unfortunately, some see these relationships as exercises in gamesmanship and as a result generate an attitude of mistrust and animosity and an atmosphere of greed and fear. Their number, however, is relatively small; the system works because trust and respect are the norms.

In the following chapters the actors in the building-construction drama are identified and explained in greater detail and their functions and interrelationships are more thoroughly defined. This exposition is necessary for a sound understanding of the economic environment in which architectural practice exists.

Architects are said to work from the general to the particular, whereas scientists are said to work from the particular to the general. Consistent with this notion is the manner in which the contents of this book are presented. It is the author's conviction that an understanding of the pond in which one is to swim is essential before one learns how to do so. If one's goal is to learn how to function as a practicing architect and to maintain that practice, it is essential to understand the nature of the larger business world in which this practice can flourish.

You are encouraged to investigate in as much depth as possible the local economy, both inside and outside the construction industry. It is hoped that an understanding and acceptance of the fact that goods and services must be paid for will emerge and that productivity, trust, and respect are valued and ultimately rewarded.

It used to be fashionable, though not very realistic, for architects to consider themselves "above" the need to function as businessmen. Fortunately, this is less true today, but it is a lesson that seems to be only reluctantly learned by many. The principles of business and management required for a successful architectural practice are to a large extent the same as those required for any other business enterprise. Therefore, it is essential for the successful architectural firm to have in its staff the highest level of business acumen possible, and it is equally essential that every architect have at least a cursory understanding of business practices and principles and a much deeper understanding of the tenets of good management, even if he is managing a one-person firm.

The American economy operates on the principle of free choice. However, when one makes a choice, one must accept responsibility for it and for its consequences. This is just as true in construction as in any other field. If one chooses to be an architect and is successful in completing the educational, practical, and registration requirements, one must accept the responsibilities and consequences of this choice. Among these are the commitment to uphold the public health, safety, and welfare; to act responsibly in regard to other people and to available resources; and, with the help of all the other players on the stage, to strive for the best work that one can produce.

2

Elements in the Construction Process

In spite of the egocentric bias of architects and other design professionals, the construction process does not start with them; in fact they often play their roles rather late in the process of a construction project.

The earliest actors—no metaphor or pun is intended; these parties are called actors because of the actions they take—are the initiators of the projects, those who decide that it is desirable, profitable, or necessary to erect a particular building or other construction. Very often they are motivated by profit; almost equally as often they are motivated by a perceived social need, as in the case of governmental officials proposing a new bridge or a new school. At times the motivation is simply personal need and desire, as in the case of a new family residence.

Sometimes the party that initiates a project does so simply because that is what it does for a living. In this case the party may be identified as a developer. Developers put "packages" together for building projects, which often include not only a site and a building but also temporary and permanent financing, leasing, and continuing maintenance. It is their business to bring together these diverse activities and perhaps "massage" (review and adjust) them until it appears that everything will work out; that is, that sufficient sales or

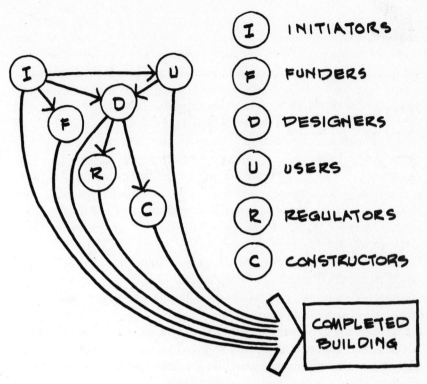

2-1 The Construction Industry

rental income can be generated to pay for the mortgage, the land, the design fees, and other expenses and still leave enough for an attractive return on investment. (The process of proving if this can be done, at least on paper, is one type of feasibility study and is discussed in more detail in Chapter 15.)

The initiator may also be an on-going business that needs more space in order to respond to a growing market. It may be a nonprofit corporate body, such as a church or a private school, that is expanding and needs additional or different kinds of space for its program of activities. Whatever the origin, the point is that someone or some group has to make the initial decision to erect a building; understanding the motivations and operational methods of this party is highly desirable if not essential in establishing and maintaining effective office practice.

The users, on the other hand, often are not the initiators. They are the people or institutions that will eventually occupy the completed project. Examples are apartment dwellers, students and teachers, office personnel, and factory workers. Frequently they have no role in the decision-making process, unless someone who does have a role involves the users directly. This appears to be a growing activity for the architect; that is, to attempt to discover and incorporate into the building design the anticipated users' ideas.

There are other parties involved in some projects. Some of these simply invest the money and allow others, such as developers, to manage the projects for them. Some are quasipublic bodies that make policy decisions which result indirectly in building projects, and some are individuals who want and perhaps need a building for a private purpose. In this last case the initiator, user, and owner may well be the same party.

For the sake of clarity, all the parties and roles described above could be grouped under the title "consumers," for in a free-market economy they are the purchasers of buildings, which are the products produced by designers and builders.

Another group that plays an early role in the construction process is the financial community, which provides money for construction and for the attendant expenses, such as design fees. This group includes not only direct lenders, such as banks, savings-and-loan associations, and insurance companies, but also private individuals, mortgage bankers, and brokers. Each has a particular set of operational features and provides loans for either or both short-term money for the development and construction period alone or, for the long-term, the mortgage, sometimes called permanent financing.

Both of these are loans and function on the basis of interest and sometimes "points" (front-end payments by the borrower of so many percentage points of the borrowed amount). In the past, interest was fixed for the life of the loan, but new loan structures with fluctuating interest rates are now a more frequently seen pattern. Both short-term and permanent loans on building projects are secured by the property (land and buildings or "improvements"), called a mortgage in the case of permanent financing. In this use the word "secured" means that, should the owner default on the loan, the lender would receive title to the property.

Occasionally the lender can demand that, in partial exchange for the service of lending the money for the project, they receive a share in the ownership of the project in addition to interest on the loan. This is sometimes called "equity."

Once a decision is made to start a project and a design team is selected, which can occur before, while, or after financing is secured, the designer's work (the initial phase of which may be necessary in order to secure financing), begins. In the discussions in this book "designer" or "designers," unless specifically noted otherwise, refers to the architect or the architectural team or firm plus the engineering and other consultants brought into the project.

A large and constantly expanding body of people and agencies plays its roles simultaneously with and as parties to the process of design. These are the regulators, bureaucrats or public officials whose task it is to administer the law as it applies to building design, location, and placement on the site and to construction details. In almost every community or local governmental jurisdiction it is necessary to secure a permit to erect a building. In order to secure a permit it is necessary to prove, through the drawings and other documents prepared for the construction, that the building will meet the legal requirements for building design and construction, as expressed in the general building, fire, plumbing, and electrical codes, and for location and other factors, as expressed in the local zoning ordinances.

Other public officials have roles to play during and after the construction of a building. When the construction documents have been completed and approved by governmental authorities, construction can begin. A general term in current use for one involved with construction is "constructor." Others are "contractor," "building contractor," "builder," and "construction company." A firm can range from a single-person operation with a pickup truck for an office and a hip pocket for a file to a multibillion-dollar conglormerate with sizable offices in many different cities and countries.

These are the major actors, or categories of actors, in the building process. The way they work internally and with each other is the subject of the next several chapters.

3

The Consumers

With the recent rise in importance of the consumer and of consumerism, it may be appropriate to assign the title of "consumer" to a buyer of architectural services, either directly, as the owner of a proposed single-family dwelling, or indirectly, as one who rents from someone who has made the direct payments. In an earlier day, just as it was thought unseemly to consider an architect a businessperson (and many were not), it would have been at best ungracious to consider owners and users as consumers.

There are at least two good reasons, in the author's opinion, for using the term "consumer." One is to reinforce the truth of the concept that, whatever architecture may be, architectural practice is a business and it must be viewed as such if the practice is to thrive. Understanding that those who purchase our services and use our products are consumers helps to put this concept into perspective. The second reason is that a term is needed that properly depicts the breadth of the architects' responsibility to those they serve. Other terms are either too limited or already appropriated for more specific use. "Owner" is understood in general use and defined in legal documents to apply only to one who holds title to property. "User," in contraposition to "owner," is held to mean only one who actually occupies and uses a building. The two may be one and the same, but often are not. "Client" usually refers to the party who employs and pays the architect. "Developer," a party who may be any or all of the preceding, has a very specialized role to play as a "packager," so this is also too narrow a term. There is a need for an umbrella word or term under which all these concepts and roles may be clustered, and "consumer" seems to serve best.

Perhaps it would be helpful to view the consumer group in the context of the "general-to-specific" spectrum. At the most general level, and also the largest in terms of numbers of people, is the public. The architect has, as we have seen, certain responsibilities to the public at large. Some of these responsibilities have been codified into law and are administered by governmental officials. Others are what the architect perceives to be in the public interest, even if not required by law, and are probably very subjective in nature. Nevertheless, architects have or ought to have a responsibility to provide an enriching environment even for those who only see their designs as they pass by on their way to other destinations.

At the next level might be the group of people who are being represented by those with whom the architect works directly. Examples would be the students in a school (or even a whole school system), the members of a church, the patients *and* the staff of a hospital, the customers *and* the salespersons of a department store, or even the children in a family that is planning a new home.

Lastly, and most specifically, are those to whom the architect is directly, and usually contractually, responsible; this is consequently, and quite naturally, the group smallest in number and most intensely involved in the decision-making process.

Following is a discussion of the general types of consumers briefly mentioned at the beginning of this chapter. As can be observed, they are distinguished by the roles they play in the decision-design-delivery process. One particular person may in fact perform several or even all the roles described. This is probably more frequently the case than not, especially in smaller projects. It could be said that the larger the project, the greater the likelihood that the different roles identified will be played by different individuals.

In the standard contract or agreement forms published by the American Institute of Architects for both architectural services and for construction, "owner" is the term used to identify the person or party for whom the work is to be done and with whom the agreement is made. In this sense the terms "owner" and "client" are practically interchangeable. "Owner" is a conventionalized word, since in some cases the owner does not own the real property ("real property" is the legal terminology for land and any improvements thereon; "real estate" is, for all practical purposes, synonymous with real property) but only rents or leases it. However, in such a case the party still "owns" something, such as the business that is to be conducted in the building or space; so perhaps "owner" is still a logical choice. Care must be taken nonetheless in transferring this terminology to contract documents in the case of rented property, since the actual owner or landlord may object and require the use of some other term, such as "tenant."

If the owner owns the building or project or the business or institution that will occupy the space, the client pays or sees that someone pays for all services and expenses related to the project. These include design fees, document-reproduction costs, insurance, building-permit feets, title searches, construction costs, utility-tap (or connection) fees, materials testing, furnishings, landscaping, and anything else necessary to meet the requirements of the project. Many other costs might be mentioned; some of those named may be paid by the contractor or the architect, but the client eventually is responsible for all costs.

A "user" may be an owner, client, tenant, or merely a person who comes to a building during the business (or school or church) day to work and play or engage in whatever activity is performed at the location. The term may be applied to an individual as an individual or as a spokesperson for a group or, in modified grammatical form, to the group itself. Depending on the structure of the project and the architect's defined and allowed roles in it, the user may have much, little, or nothing to say about the design of the facilities. A responsible architect will make some attempt to determine what the needs of these people are and to meet them, even if the needs are not perceived by the owner.

As has been previously observed, another kind of consumer is the developer. Largely working with speculative commercial projects, the developer promotes the project by seeing a real or imagined need that could be served by constructing a building and, when the effort is successful, finds a future owner or owners for the completed facility. In the process the developer assembles land, designers, constructors, and any other specialists needed; attends to zoning conformance or variances; sees that at least interim financing is available; and expedites all other details necessary to make a project "go." In so doing, he earns and receives compensation, sometimes in the form of a fee or, perhaps more often, as a portion of the ownership of the completed project. While there are special cautions to observe with regard to tax and professional liability, for example, it is quite within the realm of possibility for an architect to function as a developer, and many have. Perhaps the best known is John Portman of Atlanta, who designed and developed the original atrium hotel, which has become in a very few years a standard and very successful building type.

In the architect's work, he may be "passed off" from reporting to the developer, in the early stages, to the future owner when the project reaches the point at which specific needs must be addressed. On the other hand, the owner may wish to leave all such details in the hands of the developer and simply pay the bills and receive the revenue generated by the completed project. This is often the case with projects developed for multiple rentals, such as office or apartment buildings, or those in which the owner in the legal sense is a large financial institution, such as an insurance company.

On occasion the owner-client with whom the architect works directly is in fact a group rather than an individual. A church building committee is an example. Numerous horror stories circulate among architects about building committees, especially those composed of church or other nonprofit clients, since they usually consist of volunteers who are amateurs in regard to architectural design or construction. (In 1966 I told a conference on church architecture that I had never known an architect who thought he was a preacher but I had known several preachers who thought they were architects. This continues to be true.) The problems attending this kind of situation require perhaps more diplomacy and tact than many architects are equipped by temperament to have. Good and sometimes assertive committee leadership will go a long way toward forestalling potential problems or smoothing out those that do arise. The wise architect will try to aid the committee chairperson by seeing that the latter is aware that such leadership is needed and by assisting in the job in every way possible, which can be a very demanding task.

Regardless of the nomenclature assigned, every consumer of architecture has a right to the architect's attention at some level. Picking one's way responsibly through the different kinds of attention and loyalties one finds with the various consumer types requires of the architect a commitment to a higher degree of integrity and perhaps simply to harder work than is the case with most occupations. It is incumbent on the architect to be conscious of the fact that the responsibilities extend beyond those required by the immediate client; to be conscious means to keep those responsibilities in mind at all times.

4

The Design Professionals

The popular image of the architect is much distorted and romanticized—in both fiction and nonfiction portrayals. On television, the great leveler, we have seen an architect playing straight man to an English butler *(Our Man Higgins)*, a zany girl *(Love on a Rooftop)*, a gaggle of smart-mouthed kids *(The Brady Bunch)*, and a horse *(Mr. Ed)*. We have been shown an architect who dropped his practice and ran off to alert the world of an invasion of aliens *(The Invaders)*. Fortunately, these depictions, even if they are barely possible, are hardly typical.

The work of a design (architectural, engineering, planning, landscape-architecture) office is complex and involves many professionals, all working in a coordinated way to achieve a common goal. Many tasks must be done, many roles played. Sometimes, when the office is small a single person does many or even all of them from time to time. In larger offices, it is often thought to be more efficient, if not more individually satisfying, to specialize tasks and roles, just as it is more efficient to produce automobiles on an assembly line where one person does the same limited-scope tasks all day, day after day. This is not to say that narrow specialization is not highly satisfying to many. Apparently it is, for much work of high value is accomplished in offices organized in this way.

17

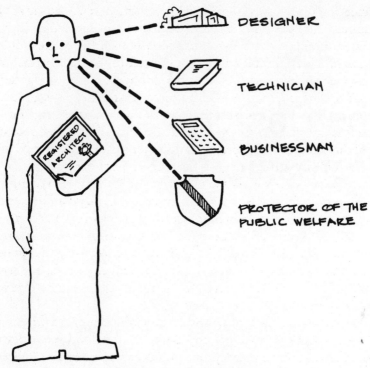

DESIGNER

TECHNICIAN

BUSINESSMAN

PROTECTOR OF THE
PUBLIC WELFARE

REGISTERED ARCHITECT

4-1   Roles of an Architect

Not all the tasks or roles in an architectural office directly relate to design of buildings or other projects. Some have to do with management in its various aspects; some with office services, such as seeing that there are adequate supplies of paper, etc., that various office machines are properly serviced, deliveries made, and so on; some are support functions—clerical, filing, and the like. However, all office activities must properly relate to the real purpose of a design office—to produce the product, or designs for buildings and the related services, in an effective and efficient way.

One way to look at the organization of an architectural office is to see how it handles engineering. There are two basic methods: to have engineers on staff (''in-house''), or to contract engineering services from independent engineering firms (consultants), usually for a specific project. Sometimes only a part of the engineering will be done by in-house staff, and other tasks will be provided by consultants.

In construction or building design there are three primary

engineering disciplines: mechanical, electrical and structural. The coordination of the work of these engineers and specialists into the "architectural" or general work is the responsibility of the architect and can be a very complex and time-consuming though critical task. (Construction drawings produced in our office are labeled "general" instead of "architectural" because these drawings are the governing or control drawings and all others are subservient to them. For the same reason, we number these drawings without prefixed letters to signal their unique and superior status among the family of drawings.)

In addition to engineering design, the primary engineers are usually responsible for cost estimating and for services during construction in their areas of work. (The work of engineers and other consultants will be discussed in more detail in Chapter 6. Office organization will be discussed in Chapter 10.) Other specialists, some of whom may not be engineers, may be involved in a particular project. These may include landscape architects, civil engineers, acoustical engineers, or interior designers. New specialities are being added with great frequency.

Depending on the type of building and the size of the project, the architect organizes the work to involve the various engineers and other specialists at the appropriate points on the schedule. For example, in a high-rise office building, or one with an unusual form, it would be typical to involve the structural engineer at an early date. If there will be unusual demands on the mechanical or electrical systems, specialists in these fields should be involved early. In general, the more complex, unusual, or costly a project is, the earlier the respective engineers and other specialists should become involved in design decisions.

However, with enough experience an architect may be able to make basic decisions in these areas and then have the engineers confirm or refine them later in the process. Especially in the early schematic-design stages, when the design is very fluid, it is often inefficient to ask the engineers to do anything more than answer a few open-ended questions that different design options may prompt.

There are certain types of projects in which the architect may not include engineers at all or only on a consultancy basis to answer a few specific questions. When architects design single-family houses the projects are very often handled in this way. Most architects who accept a commission for a house are competent in the engineering skills typically required for house design. Very daring designs may require an engineer's involvement, however, and in such case a responsible architect will employ one.

Another case in which primary engineering services may not be required is remodeling. If no structural changes are planned, a structural engineer may not be needed. This can occur in residential as well as nonresidential areas of design.

A time-honored way for architectural firms to make themselves more attractive to potential clients, especially if they have a shortcoming that might rule them out of consideration, such as small size, no experience in the particular building type, or distant location from the site, is to form a joint venture with another firm that has complementary attributes. A joint venture is a temporary business partnership formed to seek a given commission and, if successful, to perform the work for the specific project. The problems of coordination between offices as well as the division of labor, responsibility, expenses, and income can be perplexing and may make a proposed joint venture unattractive. However, much work of high value has been produced in joint ventures, and for that reason it is an option that every firm should evaluate on a case-by-case basis.

At the time they are commissioned, architectural firms may not know whether or not the tasks they have been asked to do will progress to a real construction project. These tasks, sometimes referred to as "feasibility studies," include land planning, alternative development studies, site evaluations, and, for qualified firms, the kind of predictive financial-feasibility study on land development that is usually done by realtors, developers, or mortgage bankers.

Other assignments or commissions sometimes given to architectural firms fall outside the area of building design—from urban design to furniture and graphic design, perhaps unrelated to a particular building. Some very famous and highly regarded architects such as Marcel Breuer have been known almost as much for their furniture design as for their buildings.

One fact should not be forgotten: the principal purpose and function of an architect is to design building projects—which may include more than one building but nonetheless primarily involve the design of buildings and their surroundings. Everything else must take a back seat to this, since to do otherwise is to abandon one's chosen field and enter another. An architect may do this, but if he (or she) does, perhaps he should no longer claim to be an architect.

There is no other field in which science and art are combined in such an intense and critical way. The welfare and safety of the users and of society in general depend on the careful application of science. There are other professionals and specialists who can do most of what architects take upon themselves to be responsible for, engineers particularly. However, no one else is prepared by education and motivation to provide the art, which lifts "building" to "architecture."

As mentioned in the Introduction, every participant in the design process may not have the responsibility or desire to affect design. However, all should be sympathetic toward design goals and should be able to take pride in their participation in successful projects.

5

The Constructors

As was explained in Chapter 2, the term "constructor" is an umbrella term chosen to refer to all those engaged in building contracting. In this and following chapters other terms such as "contractor" may be used interchangeably.

Construction involves the assembling of labor forces and materials required for a project and organizing the work and placement of materials in a timely manner to produce a completed building or other construction. Those entities engaged in construction come in all sizes of business, from very small to very large. It is a truism to say that the larger a project, the larger the work force and the more complex the tasks necessary to complete it. The organizational complexity probably increases on a geometric curve, while the work force may increase at a declining rate, since large projects may make greater efficiency possible.

There are numerous management tools available to the constructor to make his job easier. Some are the same as for any business involving large numbers of people or large quantities of materials. Others are specifically designed or adapted for the construction process. One of the more recent is the fine-tuned scheduling made possible through data-processing equipment, programs, and techniques.

Organizational complexity is also compounded by the fact that, in order to assure (or attempt to assure) a continuous, relatively even flow of work, a constructor is likely to be engaged in several projects at one time, each at various stages of completion. Not only must the schedule of work be planned and its progress managed for a single project, but this schedule must also be integrated into similar schedules for other projects, usually under contract for entirely different and independent owners, each with their own architects.

Most states have contractor licensing laws, which stipulate the size of project allowed (or aggregate size of all projects underway at one time). This size is parallel to and reflected by their bonding capacity, the dollar limit of a performance bond that the firm is able to purchase.

A performance bond is essentially a special insurance policy that protects the owner in case of default by the constructor. It is usually in the amount of 100 to 115 percent of the contract sum. The bond is purchased by the constructor for the owner; the constructor is reimbursed by the owner for the cost of the bond, usually about one to one and one-half percent of the contract amount, depending on the size of the contract (the larger the contract amount, the lower the percentage cost of the bond). A performance bond is not always required. If the owner knows and has confidence in the constructor to a sufficient degree, he may elect to forego the bond and thereby save that cost.

There are many categories of constructors, some who undertake almost any kind and size of project, and others, typically a majority, who tend to specialize by size or type of construction or both.

One of the more basic divisions among constructors is between those who work only or primarily in the residential market and those whose area of specialization is in the commercial (nonresidential) market. The residential market can further be subdivided into those who specialize in new single-family houses, multifamily housing, or remodeling. In commercial and other nonresidential markets there are even more subspecialties by both type and size. Among the specialties by type found among nonresidential constructors are: commercial low-rise and high-rise, health-care, retail, interior, educational, religious, recreational, industrial, remodeling, and preservation. An entire area of specialization exists that has little or no contact with architectural firms. Sometimes termed "non-building" construction, this specialty includes road building, airport (runway) construction, dam and bridge building, oil-well drilling, and pipeline laying. The design of these projects lies for the most part in the realm of civil engineering.

A typical small contractor may work in both residential and nonresidential areas in order to maintain a more uniform work flow. He may undertake residential remodelings or additions at the same time as he is working on small, freestanding commercial buildings, such as a branch bank. The skills and management tasks required will not differ greatly. The number of subcontractors needed will be similar, although not necessarily all in the same trades. This illustrates the notion that, even if he undertakes diverse types of projects, a contractor may still choose to limit his work by the level of managerial complexity required. In other words, he chooses, consciously or not, projects that have a similar level of managerial complexity.

At the opposite end of the spectrum are the giant firms, often operating internationally, which sometimes include in their operations the erection of entire temporary cities in remote places to house their work force during the lifetime of the project.

While some large construction firms extend their work over a wide geographic area, most limit their range to a state or region of the nation. Distance complicates and multiplies management and logistics difficulties, and each firm must determine for itself when a point of diminishing returns will be reached.

Some projects are so large, or require such special areas of skill, that no one firm is likely to provide all that is needed. In such cases a frequent response is for two or more firms to form a joint venture, a temporary partnership for the execution of a specific project.

Just as architectural firms sometimes form joint ventures, specialize by type and/or size of project, and limit their geographic area, so do constructors follow parallel patterns. This perhaps illustrates the interdependence of designers and deliverers in the construction industry; that is, similar operational and organizational patterns tend to evolve. At its most general and elementary level it is a symbiotic relationship, since neither group could survive without the other. To carry the analogy too far, however, would lead to misconceptions, since each group has complementary but not identical goals and values. At times some of the goals and values may even be in direct opposition.

Since continuous cooperation is essential, perhaps the responsible posture for both designer and constructor is to try to maximize the efforts and occasions for mutual aid and to try to limit the fields of disagreement. Such an attitude has not always been in favor. In the recent past the relationship was frequently more adversarial and often filled with distrust and bitterness. As the industry and its participating parties have matured, such an attitude has subsided and one of more mutual respect has evolved. This is not to say, however, that the relationship should be so close as to erase the distinctiveness of the respective roles and channels of responsibility, communication, and authority. An "arms-length" relationship must be maintained, particularly when both designer and constructor are under separate contracts to a single third-party owner. It is easy to slip into a casual camaraderie on the job site, which makes it difficult to enforce decisions on the quality of workmanship and carry out similar responsibilities contractually assigned to the architect.

Care must also be taken to avoid any possible "indebtedness" or conflict of interest due to favors, gifts, or special considerations from constructors. Architects are not without guilt in their relations with their constructor friends. When undertaking a project at their home or office, too often architects have imposed on a contractor or material supplier for cut rates or gifts of "samples." This not only hurts the giving party by cutting into profit but it has at least two other adverse effects: it establishes an indebtedness, which may be "called in" at an embarrassing or compromising time, and it undermines the moral integrity of the architect in the eyes of the other party, even if the gift is denied.

One common practice, which probably involves no impropriety, is for materials suppliers to offer architects the same discounts they give to contractors. As long as the same rates apply to all members of both groups, there should be little opportunity for abuse and no concern for conflict of interest. The suppliers have to expect a certain amount of promotional cost to encourage the purchaser (constructor) and specifier (architect) to use their products. One way this is done is through discounting, which is usually dependent upon being paid within a specified time period.

Constructors are found in many types and sizes and in even greater variety than architects. The relationships architects have with them may extend beyond the contractual into tricky depths. Architects must constantly watch that they maintain their proper role as the owner's agent and as professionals whose responsibility to some degree encompasses the whole of society.

A word needs to be said about a recurrent practice popularly called "design-build." In the years prior to the Civil War the general practice of construction was much closer to design-build than to what we now consider the orthodox tripartite structure, featuring independent owner, architect, and constructor. The story of the design and construction of the Tennessee State Capitol in Nashville is a good example. William Strickland, who had already won fame as a successful Philadelphia architect, the designer of the U.S. Mint and several other prominent buildings, was hired in 1845 to not only design the Capitol, but also "supervise the construction," which in those days meant practically the same as we now mean by "general contractor." He hired individual tradesmen, such as masons, carpenters, and roofers; he purchased materials and kept the financial records of the project (see Wilbur Creighton, *Building of Nashville*).

Design-build is not, therefore, new in the sense that one party performs both design and construction services. As practiced today the constructor usually provides the design services as part of his overall responsibility. He may hire the architect (sometimes a nonregistered designer; state laws are at times lax about requiring a registered architect or engineer if the "owner" provides his "own plans") or he may already have architects or other designers on his staff if his volume is large enough to sustain the continuing overhead and payroll required.

An architect employed on an individual-project basis by a constructor for a design-build operation must adjust his methods and outlook. However, if personal integrity is present, no problems should occur that cannot be resolved. The first point to adjust to is that the constructor is the client and is owed the primary loyalty of the architect (within the bounds of professional ethics). A dishonest party to a contract or agreement, be it constructor, architect, or anyone else, creates problems for all other parties, and the wise architect will examine the character as well as the business reputation of a constructor for whom he may be asked to provide services, just as he should in the case of any other client. In the typical design-build project the constructor functions much like a developer in that the eventual owner and user are probably other people for whom the design-build constructor contracts to provide a building of a certain type and size for a fixed amount of money. One of the dangers of this type of operation for the eventual owner is that quality control of materials and workmanship is difficult to define prior to a detailed design; therefore, it is relatively easy for an unscrupulous design-build contractor to manipulate quality in order to receive higher profits. Examples of such abuse are probably rare, but nevertheless the possibility underscores the need for the good business and commonsense practice of knowing the people with whom one makes agreements, whether they be owner, constructor, or architect.

6

Consultants, Specialists, and Other Participants

The three primary engineering disciplines involved in architectural design are structural, mechanical (plumbing and heating, ventilating, and air conditioning, or HVAC) and electrical. Unless an architectural firm has on its payroll engineers qualified in these specialties, it must engage consultants for these services, usually on an individual-project basis.

The architect's relations with these consultants is contractually similar to the client-architect relationship; there is even a standard AIA form for an architect-engineer agreement. The consultant is responsible to the architect in a similar way to that in which the architect is responsible to the client.

Consultants' services include preliminary and detailed design, production of construction documents, estimating, and services during construction. In most situations, as prime contractor with the client the architect is responsible for not only his own actions but also those of his consultants. The architect must do his utmost to make sure that not only his own services are complete and without error, but also those of his consultants. Coordinating the work and hardware of the various specialists is a demanding and crucial task and cannot be delegated or left to the hope that each consultant will fully coordinate his work with that of all other consultants and of the architect. Responsible consultants will make every effort to do so, but this still does not relieve the architect of ultimate responsibility for complete, accurate, and totally integrated design and documentation.

Almost every architect has had on at least one occasion to work out on the job site a conflict between a beam and a duct. Sometimes this cannot be done at such a late date without considerable extra cost, and the architect is held responsible for it. A few such cases can add up to bankruptcy. For this reason alone, thorough checking of drawings and specifications becomes absolutely mandatory.

There is a traditional order of construction drawings, which may be accidental but more likely has evolved from the order in which the need for each consultant was first identified or from the order in which they were first brought in for consultation in a typical project. This order is often architectural, or general; structural; mechanical; and electrical. While this order might be changed for good reason, no established practice should be abandoned capriciously. The people in the field or on the construction site might be confused by a different or unexpected order in the documentation, which could result in delay and increased cost.

Though architectural students usually take several college courses in structural analysis and design, they are not expected to perform this kind of task to any great extent in practice. Engineers specializing in structural design receive much more instruction and, since they are not responsible for the design of an entire building and all its systems, can concentrate on their own specialty, bringing to it a much greater depth of understanding. The same can be said of the other two major engineering disciplines, though architectural students traditionally receive a much larger amount of instruction in the structural field than in the fields of mechanical or electrical design.

The structural engineer's work involves an analysis of what the building's structure must do—what it must support, what external forces it must resist. The engineer must select the appropriate system for the job, and create a detailed design of that system to fit the specific needs of the project. More often than not, the basic fabric of the building shell and its internal elements will provide at least a part of what is needed for structural purposes. A frequent example is the masonry-bearing wall, which can be an exterior or interior element. This demonstrates the close interdependence between the architect and the structural engineer in arriving at an optimum design solution. Too often structural questions are left unaddressed until the schematic design has been perfected and a commitment made to it, at least on an emotional level.

Well-qualified and imaginative structural engineers can make enormously valuable contributions to the success of a design. They can identify and help evaluate alternatives from the viewpoint of efficiency, compatibility with the design objectives, and cost. Often the basic character of a building is largely determined by its structural system. In the recent past bold structural expression was thought to be required for a building to qualify as "modern architecture." Fortunately, the profession has progressed to a level of maturity that allows a wider range of design concepts and expressions. Nonetheless, it cannot be stressed too strongly that thorough integration of structural design into total design is necessary for successful architecture.

When the design for a project first begins to crystallize, structural questions should begin to be addressed. Tentative answers can then serve as a basis for further study; they may change but at least they will ensure that the appropriate questions have not been ignored only to surface later when less latitude is available. These early, tentative answers may not even be supplied by an engineer. The experienced architect may reach a point when, perhaps intuitively, he can integrate structural as well as mechanical and electrical concerns into his thinking and conceptualizing process.

Depending on the nature and complexity of the project, the structural engineer may not be formally consulted until somewhat later in the design process. The responsible architect will know through experience the opportune time to take this step. When it is taken, the engineer must be allowed to apply his training and experience fully to the tasks at hand. This does not mean that the architect should not challenge and object when he deems it proper, nor that in every case the engineer's recommended approach should be accepted. What it does mean is that the architect should listen objectively and respectfully to the engineer's thinking and recommendations and, once basic choices have been made, allow the engineer to perfect the detailed structural design.

Much of what has been said about structural design can also be said of the other fields, though each has its own unique concerns.

Mechanical engineering encompasses two distinct systems,

linked by little more than some overlap in hardware and the fact that training and traditional practice have prepared the same people to design both. The two divisions of mechanical engineering are plumbing; and heating, ventilating and air conditioning (HVAC), or environmental control. Some HVAC systems require piping for delivery of a heated or cooled medium or for central subsystems and therefore overlap with plumbing; otherwise they have little more in common than do HVAC and electrical work. Indeed, the controls, pumps, fans, and other elements of HVAC systems are becoming increasingly electrical and/or electronic in nature.

While new and perhaps drastically different plumbing, HVAC, and electrical systems will be developed, some aspects will not change so fast as others, in part because they are linked to larger systems outside the individual building or building complex, the utilities, or water, sewer, and energy-delivery systems. There is a trend toward self-contained sewer and water-recycling systems and on-site conversion of a single energy source to meet all needs. This means less dependence on external systems, though not, at least in most cases, total independence. Even so, if such independence develops at all, it will probably never be total for the single reason that society has so large an investment in existing systems and so large an inventory of useful buildings that can be upgraded periodically that it would not be cost-effective to abandon them.

Humans need clean, potable water and a mechanism to get rid of soiled waste water. They need light; they need heat in cold months and cooling in warm months. As long as architecture is defined as buildings for human occupancy, these needs must be addressed and met, and the type of hardware now in place for doing so will dominate our thinking for a long time to come.

On the other hand, changes will come, knowledge will grow, and new materials, processes, and systems will continue to be developed. The successful design practitioner will structure his practice and design thinking to allow changes in all these areas to be integrated with ease and with the fullest usefulness.

Electrical work includes not only the systems of delivery and application of electrical power for lighting and for equipment of various kinds but also human-to-human, human-to-machine, and machine-to-machine communication systems. Some communication systems are contained within a building or cluster of buildings and some are linked with external elements, such as that between a fire alarm system and the fire department or the ubiquitous telephone system. Computer hardware is largely communicative in nature and will more and more become a part of the human scene. Providing for not only the present level of use but also for growth in the use of data processing is one of the more critical challenges facing the design profession. Detailed design of a building's electronic system is a major part of the electrical engineer's work.

Because of the increasing integration of mechanical and electrical work, there is a trend toward consulting firms offering services in both fields. Care must be taken in dealing with such firms to ensure that their design and practice attitudes are truly integrated and not just a case in which both disciplines are located for management purposes in the same firm, with little or no coordination between them.

Working with engineers requires tact and firmness. It is easy for an engineer whose discipline focuses on only a narrow part of the entire design problem to lose sight of the more basic objectives and sometimes of the budget. One of the architect's thankless but critical tasks is to maintain a proper balance in the level of quality and therefore cost among the various building systems. "Gold-plating" one part of a project is an easy trap to slip into if one is not responsible for the whole project. For this reason it is wise to make the consultants feel responsible for the whole project. Most of them are receptive and sympathetic to these goals when they are fully informed about the budget and other constraints and objectives the architect may have.

Consultants also need to be fully informed about schedules. Because outside (as opposed to "in-house") consultants have other projects, probably for other architects, scheduling becomes very difficult and increasingly crucial as the size of the project increases. To call in a consultant at the last minute and ask for immediate delivery of a completed design and documents is unrealistic and unfair. Even if a realistic time period is given for the work on an individual project, it may not be feasible given the other work to which the consultant is also committed. Therefore, schedule planning as far in advance as possible is the best practice, even if the demands of the client sometimes prevent or circumvent it.

There are many other kinds of consultant fields, which are dealt with in a similar fashion to that of the major disciplines already discussed. Some of these specialties are: civil engineering, landscape architecture, interior design, acoustical design, theatrical design, security, data processing, and an increasing number of specialists in specific building types, such as health-care and criminal-justice facilities. Some are useful for a wide range of projects and some only to a specific building type. Some are subspecialties of the major disciplines and others are essentially separate from them. What must be remembered is that in building design all must be orchestrated, controlled, and coordinated by the generalist, the architect.

7

Governmental Authorities

At each level of government there are agencies with authority over building design or location or both. Sometimes, with a particular building type, there may be a completely different set of offices or bureaus that has authority over certain aspects of a project.

Of the three fundamental levels of government—local, state, and federal—the first, local, has the most direct impact on building design; usually it is the only one of the three with jurisdiction over building location. This comes under the heading of zoning; design and construction are governed by building codes.

"Local" government can encompass two overlapping sets of laws and regulations, one imposed by the city, the other by the county. Usually, however, one of the two grants jurisdiction to the other. The recent trend toward unified city-county governments, as in Indianapolis, Jacksonville, and Nashville, has made the approval process somewhat simpler in those locations.

Zoning regulations essentially control where in a city specific types and uses of property may occur, minimum lot sizes and setbacks, density (dwelling units per acre), ground cover, and the like; all are designed to ensure that land development occurs in conformance with a jurisdiction-wide plan that has been approved by society, acting through its government. Building codes control the quality of con-

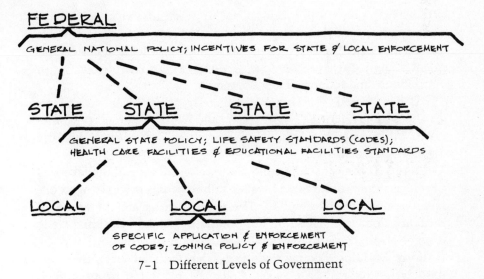

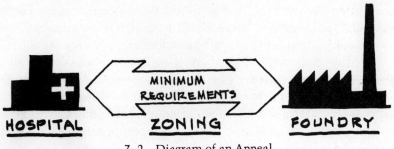

7-1   Different Levels of Government

struction with regard to protection from such hazards as fire, earth-quake, overloading, or freezing.

Zoning is designed to assure that adjacent land uses are compatible and complementary. It seeks to prevent, for example, placing a tannery and a housing development or a foundry and a hospital side by side. The characteristics of a tannery include a particularly unpleasant odor, which no one would choose to live near; the noise and smoke created by a foundry would tend to disturb the hospital patients. Zoning also attempts to ensure that adequate parking is available for any use and that the streets serving a proposed building project are adequate for the traffic the project will generate.

Progressive zoning ordinances often contain provisions for planned unit developments (PUD), in which, if a minimum amount

7-2   Diagram of an Appeal

of land is assembled and developed as a unit, within that development certain leeway and flexibility is permitted as long as overall densities and certain other types of criteria fall within specific limits. Most frequently applied to housing developments, PUDs may also occur in commercial and industrial developments.

Different sets of criteria are usually provided in zoning ordinances for residential, commercial, and industrial property; sometimes other categories are defined, such as agricultural, historic districts, and institutional uses.

Building codes usually conform with one of several model codes developed and promulgated by quasipublic bodies originating in different regions of the country. The most popular are the Standard Building Code (published by the Southern Standard Building Code Congress), the Building Officials Code Authority (BOCA), and the Uniform Building Code. In addition, the National Fire Protective Association (NFPA) Life Safety Code 101 has often been adopted parallel with the building code. This code specifically focuses on safety from fire and has been developed by people involved in fire protection—fire-department officials and the fire-insurance industry.

Building codes specify such matters as the acceptable fire resistance of materials and of assemblies of materials; exiting methods and capacities; openings in walls, floors, and roofs; and allowable heights of buildings of differing construction types. A thorough study and understanding of building codes is essential to becoming an architect.

To make a building code a part of local law, the legislative or appointive body will adopt by official action one of the model codes, possibly with some local variations. It is also possible that both a building code and the NFPA Life Safety Code will be adopted, with the more restrictive provisions applying in case of conflict.

The most frequent form of administration for both codes and zoning is through an agency, often called the ''building department,'' but more likely with a more officious-sounding name. There may be two separate departments—one for zoning and one for building. In addition, approvals must usually be secured from separate departments overseeing plumbing, fire safety (the Fire Marshall), and public works (curbs, walks, storm drainage), which connect the publicly owned infrastructure and perhaps other private systems. The procedure is for the owner to apply for a building permit. This may be done by the owner himself or by the architect, but is usually handled by the general contractor when complete construction documents are in hand and a construction contract has been signed. The dollar amount of the construction contract is important because it is often the basis on which building-permit fees are determined. Once the application has been filed, drawings and specifications are given to the various departments for review. The process may take anywhere from a few days to several weeks, depending on the complexity of the job and the efficiency of the bureaucracy.

If in the review process a deficiency is found, the party filing the application is notified and given the opportunity to either revise the documents or to file for an appeal. Appeals are usually handled by a panel of citizens (not governmental employees), which may meet at weekly to monthly intervals and often has final authority. These panels are called "appeal boards." Their hearings are usually open to the public, but their deliberations are more likely to be in closed session.

In actual practice, the architect often seeks an informal review prior to completion of the design so any revisions required can be made at that time. The opinions received in such reviews may not be binding but can usually be accepted as factual and acted upon. There are times when the owner and architect know that a nonconforming condition is being planned and that it will have to be appealed. In such cases a building permit may be applied for prior to the completion of the documents; if it is rejected, an appeal is then filed. A fee is charged for appeal, but the building-permit fee is not payable until the permit is granted. However, some governments may have a review fee and certain other kinds of fees, which might be due at different times.

In zoning appeals there are basically two positive actions possible—a variance, which allows nonconforming use for what the appeals board deems good and sufficient reason, or a zoning change, in which it is necessary to modify the official city or county-wide zoning map. Obviously, the latter is the more time-consuming and difficult; it usually needs the approval of not only the zoning appeals board but also the local legislative body, such as the city council. Appeals of zoning matters are usually accompanied by a review by the city or county planning office or commission. This agency is the staff sup-

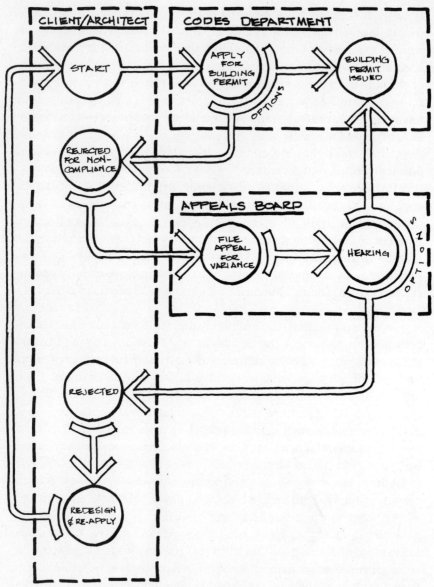

7-3   Zoning

porting the zoning appeals board and has produced the jurisdiction-wide zoning and land use and development plan. It publishes the regulations governing zoning matters, the zoning ordinance.

    The higher the level of government, the more the likelihood that the law affecting building will be directed toward public policy than toward specifics of safety or public welfare. A state may adopt a building code but leave its administration to the local government. State governments often have a fire marshall's office, which has review authority only over certain building types, such as health-care facilities or federally funded and state- or local-government-administered projects, or over sprinklers and certain other fire-safety-related systems.

Many states have an environmental-protection agency and a department of public health, both of which may review such projects as sewage treatment facilities and industrial plants that discharge potentially hazardous materials. There may be a state energy agency; most states have adopted some form of energy-conservation code.

There are other special-focus codes, which may be purely local or statewide. These often include occupational safety and handicapped-accessibility codes. Again, these are usually adopted by the state government as public policy but administered by local government.

The developers of all health-care facilities in which patients are kept overnight—hospitals, nursing homes, extended-care facilities—have to secure a "certificate of need" from a state agency. The petition passes through a series of local-to-state review panels, which determine if there is an existing or anticipated need for the beds that the proposed facility will add to the total inventory in the local area, the district, and the state. This process carries out the public policy that no surpluses of costly health-care facilities occur.

Educational facilities fall under another set of state laws directed toward maintaining a minimum level of educational quality. These laws are superimposed on local building codes and zoning ordinances and probably apply to both public and private educational institutions.

The federal government's role in specific building-design regulation is minimal, unless it is involved in funding, insuring, or actually owning the project.

In 1970 the Occupational Safety and Health Act (OSHA) was passed; at first it appeared as if it would in effect become a national building code. While OSHA has no doubt had an impact on building design, except for industrial and other facilities with large numbers of employees or highly hazardous environments it has not been of very serious concern in building design, and no mechanism exists for federal enforcement of its provisions during the building-design process. For most common building types the applicable building codes have comparable requirements; following these requirements will usually satisfy all OSHA requirements.

Making one's way through the thickets of government agencies and approvals is not only a difficult and tricky task but also a life-long quest. Each locality handles matters a little differently. It is easy to drift into a posture of confrontation with building officials and to come to the point of believing that their only function and greatest pleasure is to make life difficult for architects and contractors. While there will always be the occasional misfit, grouch or incompetent in a position of authority in a building department or governmental agency, the great majority are conscientious, well-meaning, and co-operative people, especially if treated with respect and good humor. One would be well advised to keep everything "up front" and to avoid trying to play games with the approval process. Rather than finding oneself in an adversary position with public officials and government employees, it is much more productive to promote an atmosphere of helpful cooperation among all parties.

8

Codes, Ordinances, and Other Legal Considerations

The content and intent of building codes and zoning ordinances have been rather thoroughly described in the preceding chapter. However, further emphasis might profitably be placed on their role in the construction industry.

Registered or licensed professional designers, in other words architects and engineers, have a legal obligation to design all their projects to meet the requirements of applicable codes and ordinances. Even if the client requests a deviation, the architect or engineer must, to the best of his knowledge, belief, and ability, honor the legal obligation. To do otherwise would subject him to several types of serious risk. One possibility is loss of registration and therefore the means of livelihood. Another is exposure to liability or to civil or criminal action should any accident, failure or injury occur which can be shown to relate to a design that does not conform to codes. In addition, it is possible, though not likely, to face legal action for simply producing a nonconforming design even when no injury occurs.

As has been noted earlier, mechanisms are usually available through which variances from strict legal requirements can be sought when good and sufficient reason can be shown. In the case of building-code variances, such relief often requires providing other, nonmandatory features that, in the eyes of the reviewing authority, provide equal or greater protection than the feature to be deleted.

It will be shown in later chapters that the work of a design professional encompasses much more than design. In certain contracted relationships, the architect's verbal instructions to the constructor can in effect modify the terms of the contract. Therefore, the architect needs to exercise great care not only in what he says on a job site but also in controlling what others representing his firm may say. Carelessness in this kind of situation can mean that the architect will be required to pay for some work involved in the project; this can occur if, for example, he inadvertently leads the constructor to believe that approval for a change has been granted so that, due to time constraints, work can proceed in advance of a formal, written change order. If the owner does not agree to the change, which may have already been completed, the architect may be responsible for not only the cost of the change but also the cost of removing the revised work or restoring the project to its originally intended condition.

The architect performs his work under a professional-services agreement. This may be and often is the AIA (American Institute of Architects) Standard Form of Agreement Between Owner and Architect (currently either AIA Document B141 or B161) in which pertinent data such as identifications of the owner, architect, and project are inserted, as are the financial terms and other special provisions. Other agreement forms may be used; governmental agencies often have their own standard forms for professional-services agreements. An agreement may also be a simple letter or even totally verbal, although it is always wise to put agreements in writing so that any later disagreements will have some commonly accepted and understood basis for resolution.

The important point, however, is that, no matter which form for services is used, the architect is obligated legally and ethically to fulfill its requirements. Though generally not a signatory to the construction contract, the architect is usually assigned certain roles and relationships by it. In the typical construction contract the constructor is required to do certain things with and through the architect and to secure the architect's approval on a number of key items and milestones in the progress of the building.

There are two frequently used forms published by the AIA, one for typical medium-and-up-sized projects (AIA Document A101) and another, somewhat simpler form for smaller projects (AIA Document A107). The AIA also publishes a separate document called "General Conditions to the Construction Contract" ("General Conditions" for short, AIA Document A201), which in the typical project is included by reference in the construction contract. The contract form for smaller projects contains in its text a similar but briefer set of general conditions.

That part of the contract document, popularly known as "specifications," usually contains matter other than specifications, such as Instructions to Bidders; a summary of the work of the project; general requirements having to do with such matters as temporary facilities, cleanup, and processing of submittals; General Conditions; and Supplementary Conditions, which modify the General Conditions to meet the specific needs of the project. These, along with the specifications, are usually printed in a bound volume. The preferred term for this volume is "Project Manual," since it contains more than specifications. It is an integral, vital, and complementary part of the construction contract, along with the working drawings and the contract itself. Because they have been included in the construction contract, the sheets of drawings, then, must be considered as legal documents. They must be clear, concise, unambiguous, and easily understood. Wording in notes, schedules, and legends likewise must not only be clear and unambiguous but also easy to read and to relate to the graphic material.

The object and purpose of the working drawings are to illustrate what is to be constructed; they establish the scope of the project. The specifications, on the other hand, establish the quality of materials and workmanship required for the project.

Part II

PROFESSIONAL ORGANIZATION, MANAGEMENT, AND PROCEDURE

9

The Professional Design Office

The most general and therefore the least informative role of the professional design office is, of course, to design buildings. With that out of the way, a more sober look at the discrete tasks and responsibilities usually necessary to accomplish that worthy goal is now possible and desirable. These are summarized here and dealt with in greater detail in following chapters.

The division of labor and organization of tasks in a design office reflect to some extent the management philosophy and notions of the principals, to some extent the realities of the marketplace, in many respects the historical period in which the office operates, and most assuredly the nature of the major work (projects) produced by that office.

However, no matter how large or small the firm, whatever its organizational pattern or geographic location, certain broad categories of labor and responsibility are almost universal. In no order of importance these include marketing, administration, design, production, and contract administration. Others, which allow more variation or option, may include specialized design (such as interiors), in-house engineering, and various support functions for the design component, such as model building or photography.

In a small office all tasks may be performed by everyone, or even

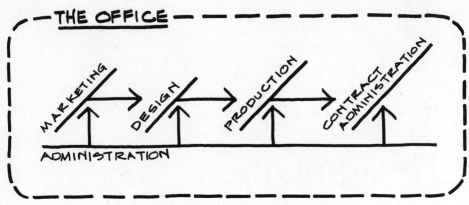

9-1   Divisions of Labor in Design Offices

by the same person in a one-person office. This is not at all rare: each
year many new offices are started by one person with an answering
service, all or most expecting to grow quickly beyond that meager
level.

MARKETING

A few years ago marketing might properly have been considered
as part of administration. Indeed, during the first two decades after
World War II, expansion in the building industry was so rapid and continuous that, except during a few recessionary periods, few firms had
to consider marketing at all in any formal sense. The principal simply
maintained the proper contacts among the local civic leaders. When-
ever a public or large private project would come up, he would auto-
matically be considered and would receive an adequate share of the
total work. If a group such as a church decided to build a building, the
building-committee chairman would call in the architects he knew
for informal interviews. If he did not know any, he would ask some of
his friends to recommend one or more.

This procedure did not prevent objective and thoughtful selections to be made on the basis of merit; it merely was the process by
which one initially got on the list of architects to be considered. It is
still used, though supplemented by more modern and sophisticated
methods. Even today, most work comes to offices by referrals and
from repeating clients.

Since the mid-1960s, however, the market for architects has become much more competitive, and marketing has emerged as a separate, critically necessary, and highly complex task. It now has its own professional association and hardly a month goes by when a marketing seminar does not take place somewhere in the nation. Several excellent books have been written on this subject (see the Bibliography), which can be helpful in understanding both the need for and the methods of marketing. It is one of the evolving specialties that may be attractive to some architects who feel the need to get out of the office more or who simply have the skills and temperament for sales. For despite what some marketing experts may claim, that's what it is—selling.

Marketing theory for design offices requires a marketing plan or strategy. This plan should identify large categories of building types or "markets." It might also identify as markets consumer groups or owners who build more than one type of building. These markets are then analyzed for projected activities in the firm's preferred geographical area over the next year or other selected period. The analysis is designed to ascertain the desirability to the firm of doing the projects and its ability not only to do them but to demonstrate to a prospective client that it can competently design that kind of building. After data have been gathered and analyzed, a selection is made of the most likely "markets," and work proceeds to uncover "leads" (advance information on a possible project) and to follow up on them.

The person who manages the marketing program of a design firm closely parallels in approach and organization a sales manager in a different kind of business organization. The sales manager manages; salespeople sell. This is to some degree true in architectural firms, since all principals and almost all professionals should be and are involved in the marketing program if it is to be successful. A good marketing plan allows for and encourages the development of opportunities arising from unexpected sources; but marketing, just like design and production planning, must proceed along orderly lines and work toward established and acknowledged goals, not simply windfalls.

At first glance it might seem strange to place marketing before other tasks, but there is a reason. In manufacturing businesses, or those that are product- rather than service-related, it would be normal to consider marketing after or at least simultaneously with production. The difference is that architecture is a service, not a product, and production cannot begin until after the sale has established what is to be produced. If marketing is not successful no production will occur.

ADMINISTRATION

Administration is that cluster of tasks which keeps the office running so that the work can be done. Included are bookkeeping, disbursements, inventory of supplies, setting and administering personnel policies, assigning space, housecleaning, and managing all the above. If the firm is small, one principal may be the designated business manager and devote a portion of his time each week to these responsibilities. Large firms can require entire departments, involving no direct participation by a principal at all except to receive and approve periodic reports.

In brief, administration includes all the tasks and responsibilities that cannot be assigned to specific design projects or to prospective projects (marketing). In this sense it parallels the division of time and other expenses noted as indirect, whereas direct time and expenses relate to specific projects. A more fully developed discussion of these concepts is found in a later chapter.

DESIGN

For the architectural student the concept of design is no doubt easy to grasp, and any discussion of design per se would be repetitive at best and very likely counterproductive; it is a subject already excluded from the scope of this book. However, it is useful to discuss the place of design in the spectrum of total tasks to be accomplished by an architectural firm and its relation to other work. In short, how is "design" managed?

In larger firms the design function may be assigned to younger people who have shown marked ability. They may be grouped in one separate department or individually assigned to different project teams. Their concepts are reviewed on a more or less formal basis by the supervisors and ultimately by one or all principals. Eventually, an approved concept is developed and presentation drawings and/or a model are produced to show to the client.

The smaller the firm, the less rigid and formalized the structure under which the process just described takes place. The process, however, is basically the same; only the "designer" changes. A corollary might be that the smaller the firm, the more likely that the design function is actually performed if not supervised by a principal. The difficulties some firms have had in growing are sometimes due to the pattern in which a particular principal is the firm's only "designer," who has difficulty delegating any of his work to subordinates.

To summarize, by whatever internal processes are used, a "designer" must come up with a design concept for the project; it must then be refined and developed until it is ready to be presented to the client; and a presentation must be produced. All of these tasks may be the work of one person; but, if the firm cares about the quality of its output, the principals and perhaps others will be involved to some degree, depending on the size of the firm and its organizational structure.

Beyond that point, the actual presentation must be made and approval of the client received before the project can be moved into the production phase. This may require only one more or less formal presentation with a few minor revisions, but it is more likely that the project will be sent "back to the board" for major revision one or more times, with new presentations each time; occasionally the initial design will be completely scrapped and the team will be asked to start over. Every firm has probably had a few projects that were terminated in the design phase simply because the designers could not come up with a concept that the client considered suitable. This is only one reason why a project may be terminated at this point and probably one of the less frequent ones. However, it does happen and it serves to remind the sensitive designer that he is not omniscient, that it is not possible to please every client, and that humility is a necessary human quality.

PRODUCTION

After approval of the design, the project moves into the production phase. In most cases, this occurs by way of a transitional phase, identified in the AIA Standard Form of Agreement as Design Development. In any event, at the proper point production of the construction documents begins; they are called "documents" because they consist of written matter—specifications, conditions, bidding instructions, etc.—as well as drawings. This phase involves more work, especially in terms of man-hours, than any of the other phases formalized in the AIA Standard Form of Agreement, usually representing 40 percent of the total compensation.

CONTRACT ADMINISTRATION

When the contract documents have been completed and approved by the client, and a construction contract has been secured by written negotiation or bidding, construction of the project can begin and the work of the designing firm moves into the final phase. In the language of most professional-services agreements it is currently called Contract Administration or Services During Construction.

Traditionally this work has been called "supervision." However, courts have ruled in several cases over the last two or three decades that the term "supervision" means more than architects intended it to mean. As a result, a few architects have been faced with sizable judgments rendered against them because a court found that they did not properly "supervise" a project and an adverse event occurred on that project injuring some party. Since about 1960 the word "supervision" usually has not been used in professional-services agreements; other terms such as mentioned above have been adopted that more accurately describe the actual responsibilities the architect intends to assume.

Whatever it is called, the work of this phase is to represent the Client-Owner during the construction period, performing certain tasks, which tend but do not guarantee to assure that the project will be built according to the terms of the construction contract, of which the construction documents are a part. In addition, the architect assists the constructor and Owner in a variety of ways, including interpretation of the documents, working out unforseen problems occurring on the job, checking submittals (shop drawings, catalog information on equipment to be installed, and material samples), preparing and processing change orders, and certifying pay requests.

The general progress and quality of the project are checked periodically by the architect's designated inspectors and by those representing the various engineering disciplines. Progress is compared to a proposed schedule submitted by the constructor at the commencement of the work; if actual progress does not match that projected by the schedule, the architect may take steps to determine the reasons and, if possible, to discover how to get the project back on schedule. Occasionally, delays occur due to weather, strikes, or what is sometimes called "an act of God"; no one is to blame and nothing can be done but to accept the lost time and make the best of the situation. In some cases, the construction contract includes a penalty clause in which the contractor is penalized a stipulated amoung of money for each day (week or month) the completion of the project is delayed beyond a specified date. The legal term for this kind of provision is "liquidated damages." In even rarer cases, the construction contract has included a bonus for completing a project ahead of schedule.

The final action by a design office is the project closeout. This begins with the final inspection and ends with the acceptance of the building by the owner, with all work completed in an acceptable manner, guarantee-warranty documents and other legal instruments delivered, and final payment made.

In actual practice, of course, a great many activites color, diversify, and complicate the process just described in simplified form. The design office's involvement often does not terminate abruptly when the official project closeout takes place. Frequently "callbacks" occur, and even when the architect is in no way responsible, good public relations require him to assist in solving the problem. It can take some time, especially for first-time building owners, to learn that the quickest service on a balky piece of equipment, for example, can be obtained by calling the party who accepted responsibility for that equipment on the guarantee-warranty applying to it. It is usual to require the general contractor to guarantee the entire project for one year and for each supplier and/or subcontractor also to guarantee that part of the project for which he is responsible.

A practice that is becoming more common is for the professional-services agreement to obligate the architect to conduct one or more follow-up inspections at intervals of, for example, six, nine, and/or twelve months after completion.

In summary, the design professional's office must be prepared to work for the client from the very moment it is employed to the realization of the objective of the entire effort, a completed building project. The process described in this chapter illustrates the procedures usually followed in the construction industry.

10

Office
Organizational
Patterns

Accepting the notion that the work of a design office can be subdivided into marketing, administration, design, production, and contract administration, how should the office be organized to perform these functions effectively and efficiently?

In any size firm or type of organization there is inherently a certain amount of slack or nonproductive time. The nature of the construction industry and the American economy more or less ensure that circumstance. The objective, then, is to minimize this loss of time, which means loss of efficiency and ultimately loss of income.

Since it is axiomatic that the smaller the firm, defined by the number of persons on staff, the more activities each person will be involved in, it is critical that the best choices as to who does what be made. The smaller firm does not have the luxury of having specialists in each area and subarea, as do the larger firms. In the previous chapter, marketing was discussed rather extensively, and it is of vital importance no matter what the firm's size. However, it is unlikely that a separate staff member employed solely for marketing purposes could be justified in firms smaller than, say, twenty-five to thirty people. (The usual way to determine the size of a firm is to count only the *professional* or *technical* staff—architects, designers, draftsmen, engineers, inspectors—not clerical personnel, even though they provide a very valuable service.)

Likewise, as has been observed, it is not likely that administration could effectively occupy all the time of even one staff member, much less a principal, in a similar-size firm. The complete architect must be knowledgeable, capable, and experienced in all these areas if he aspires to be a principal. One of the benefits to an architect-in-training or a technician of working for a smaller firm is the relative ease with which exposure to and experience in all facets of practice may be attained compared with the pattern of locked-in specialization sometimes (but not always) found in larger firms.

There are two basic concepts of office organization, based on how a project flows through the firm. Neither is likely to be found in pure form except in firms large enough to afford some specialization or to carry several sizable projects simultaneously. The two types are usually called "horizontal" and "vertical."

The horizontal pattern is characterized by layers of departments, each with a rather narrowly defined scope and responsibility. There might be a department for programming (or predesign); one for design; another for presentation specialties such as model making, photography, and renderings; others for construction drawings, specifications, estimating, engineering, and so on. As a project progresses through the various phases, it is passed, literally, from one department to the next. Its progress and quality may be guided and overseen by one responsible party, such as a Project Manager or Principal-in-Charge, but it is unlikely that anyone else will maintain contact with it from start to finish.

This system works very well for some types of projects and some types of clients. However, many clients are uneasy with it and become concerned with the prospect of loss of control if the project is not handled adroitly by the responsible professional managing it.

In comparison, the vertical pattern is marked by a system of teams, which may be assembled specifically for particular projects. Each team and each member stay with the project as long as it is necessary and effective to do so. Specialists in such areas as engineering, estimating, and specifications are brought in as temporary team members when needed.

This system seems to have more potential for maintaining quality control and good client relations than does the horizontal pattern. It does, however, require tighter management in that it may be more difficult to keep all personnel effectively employed. In other words, it seems to have more potential for slack time. If the project is large

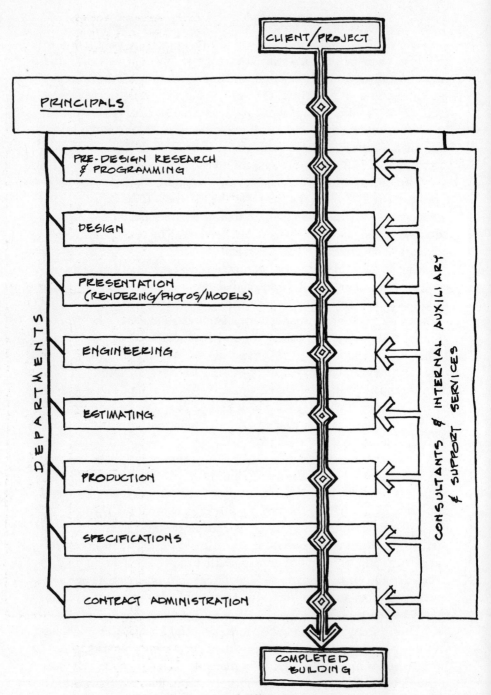

10-1A   Horizontal Office Organization

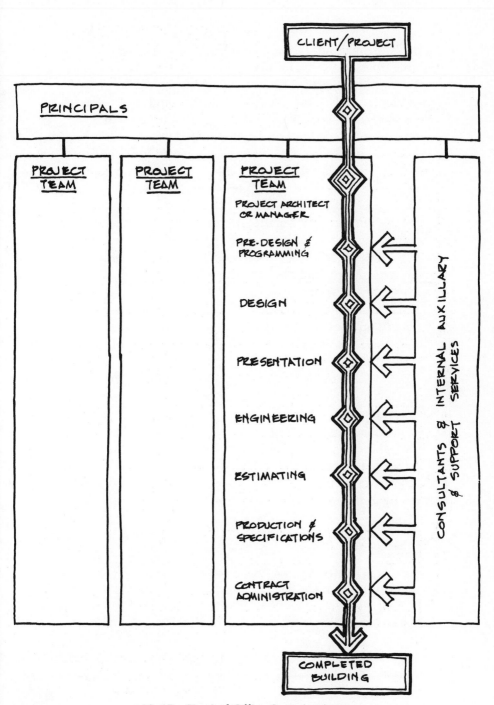

10-1B   Vertical Office Organization

enough, the team may utilize several types of technicians almost continuously throughout its life. Otherwise, and more typically, the core
team members may find themselves performing a greater variety of
tasks. In so doing there is less likelihood that critical information and
design objectives will be lost sight of than would be the case if new
people take over the work at several stages along the way.

If there is a trend in office organizational patterns, it is probably
toward the vertical type or one of its variations. Many large firms have
set up what are essentially smaller firms within a large parent organization, which is in essence the classic vertical pattern with a new
nomenclature.

For obvious reasons, smaller firms resemble the vertical pattern
rather than the horizontal. The key is to be flexible enough to respond
to whatever the needs are at the moment while maintaining sufficient
continuity, quality, and a level of stability in assignments to allow
growth and maturation in the various task areas.

There is no problem in determining an effective organizational
pattern in a one-person firm. In a two-person partnership it is necessary to establish some ground rules about who does what, but flexibility is still an ever-present commodity. As the number of principals
increases, so does the need for an organizational pattern that is clear
and also easily understood by all personnel. Great stress on the firm as
a whole and frustration on the part of employees and principals can be
wrought by hazy lines of responsibility. This condition can promote
an atmosphere of distrust, indulgence in politics, and loss of effectiveness and quality. If a technician cannot get the answer he wants
from his own supervisor, he may go to another, who might tell him
something different. It is easy to see where this can lead.

ON SELECTING PARTNERS

Partners in an architectural practice should be selected with great care,
almost as much as one takes in selecting one's spouse.

Let's examine a two-man partnership; these observations can easily
be extended to larger firms. It would do little good if two partners were exactly alike in temperament, talent, inclinations, and aspirations. Partners ought to complement, not duplicate, each other. If both see
themselves primarily as designers, for example, there will probably be
continual stress and frustration over who ''gets to'' design and who ''has
to'' do the other stuff.

If one partner is strong in design, or thinks he is and wants to be the designer partner, then the other should be strong in a complementary area, and they should agree on who will be responsible for those tasks to which neither is especially attracted. For example, partner A might be the designer and partner B the administrator. On reflection, they decide that a reasonable division of the remaining work would be as follows: production, partner A; specifications, partner B; contract administration, partner A; marketing, both. In actual practice they will probably share and participate in each other's areas, but, having agreed on who has *primary* responsibility in each area, they have made the lines clear and the stage is set for a productive relationship.

It is also advantageous if both partners are somewhat different in temperament. If both are tense, blunt, and outspoken, the tension in the office could become unbearable. If they are both calm, reserved, and diplomatic, they might find they rarely speak to each other for fear of causing stress. All these qualities have their place, but it is better if they are found in different people.

An architectural practice needs someone with imagination not only of what buildings can be built but also of what the firm can become. It also needs someone to keep the firm's feet firmly planted in reality, in the practical, the "doable." Together, prospects for a long and fulfilling practice are high.

When examined on a purely practical level, it might seem that a three-partner practice would be ideal, with one person responsible for administration, one for design, and one for production. There have been a few successful and highly visible three-partner firms, such as SOM, HOK, and CRS, but they are usually corporate giants with several office locations and many levels of partners. Like many law firms, they have simply decided to limit the legal name of the firm to the three original partners.

More often, the inherent instability of a three-partner practice surfaces and it collapses. Human frailty being what it is, situations will arise with increasing frequency in which two partners will take positions in opposition to the third and create great stress and frustration. A successful three-person partnership takes infinitely more patience, diplomacy, good sense, and luck than does a two-person partnership.

Partners should share in the dreams and goals of the practice and contribute all they possibly can toward these ends. They should be flexible and open to new possibilities and changing market circumstances, and have a positive attitude that expresses "let's find a way to do it."

There are several forms or types of firm ownership, which are described in terms of the legal position or positions of the principals.

The basic type is the sole proprietorship. This is usually at least the first stage for any architect striking out on his own and is probably

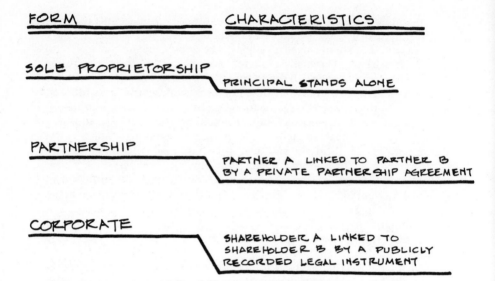

FORM   **CHARACTERISTICS**

SOLE PROPRIETORSHIP

PRINCIPAL STANDS ALONE

PARTNERSHIP

PARTNER A LINKED TO PARTNER B
BY A PRIVATE PARTNERSHIP AGREEMENT

CORPORATE

SHAREHOLDER A LINKED TO
SHAREHOLDER B BY A PUBLICLY
RECORDED LEGAL INSTRUMENT

10-2   Office Ownership Patterns

still the most prevalent form of ownership. In this form one principal owns the practice, takes responsibility for all it does, assumes all the risks, and receives as his income all the profit from the operation of the firm. The joining of two or more principals in one firm or practice constitutes a partnership, although the legal name and form may be different if they incorporate or set up the firm in one of the forms similar to incorporation legally permitted for professionals in some states, often called a professional corporation.

A sole proprietorship may be a one-person firm or one with several hundred people. Any kind of organizational pattern may be employed; the distinguishing characteristic is that the principal is solely responsible for everything related to the firm, whether it includes only himself or a staff of several hundred.

An unincorporated partnership operates in the same way as a sole proprietorship, with the exception that the partners share the responsibility, risks, and income of the practice. Unless they have entered into an agreement to do otherwise, the partners share these equally and jointly. All sorts of provisions can be included in a partnership agreement, but public accountability—those activities for which liability can be assigned if loss or injury to another party results—in most cases cannot be subdivided in an unincorporated practice. This means that each partner is liable for the actions of all partners.

In sole proprietorships and unincorporated partnerships the principals have personal tax liability for all income received from the firm. In most cases, under present law there is no advantage and some disadvantage for a sole proprietor to incorporate. In a conventional corporation the owners are responsible not only for tax on their personal income but also for tax on the income of the corporation itself, which is taxed at a different rate. Below certain levels of financial activity, measured in dollars of revenue generated per year or some similar monetary yardstick, a special type of incorporation, sometimes known as a "subchapter S" or "small business" corporation, is available. This allows the principals to be taxed in essentially the same way as they would be as individuals. To qualify, the firm has to keep the carryover cash-in-hand at the conclusion of the fiscal year below a specified level; whatever is carried over is taxed heavily.

The ramifications of incorporation are numerous and should be thoroughly explored with an attorney and a tax specialist before any decision is made. The laws constantly change and what is most advantageous this year may not be next year. The principal advantages seem to be in the areas of tax relief and pension planning, though these may not be as great as they once were. The professional corporation, usually the only type available to architects and engineers, offers little if any protection from liability when compared to unincorporated practice.

These conditions exist only in states allowing professional corporations; not all do. Some states require a separate corporate registration in addition to registration by one or all of its principals. If a loss or injury occurs on a particular project and results in a lawsuit, the legal entity that has "sealed" the documents, be it a corporation or an individual, is the one brought first into court.

Another advantage of incorporation is that it provides an easy way to transfer ownership: it is simply a matter of selling one's stock. However, in most states a stockholder in a professional corporation must be registered to practice in that state. A corollary to this advantage is that, like a sole proprietorship or a partnership, the estate of a principal is passed to his heirs at his death; if the practice is incorporated, it is relatively easy to sell the stock to a registered person, such as one of the surviving stockholders. Many incorporated practices carry a special insurance policy on the stockholders for the purpose of buying the stock of a deceased stockholder from his heirs. This not only assures the continuity of the practice by its principals, but also provides for an estate of established value for a deceased stockholder's survivors.

Not every state requires an actual architect's seal, but most do. Nevertheless, the name of the responsible party is always identified and the registration number is shown on the construction documents produced by the firm for any project reaching the construction stage. Some states require that each set of prints (not original drawings) be sealed with an embossing seal showing the name of the architect or the professional corporation, the name of the state, the words "registered architect" or a similar phrase, and the registration number. Sometimes a special device or design specified by the state is made an integral part of the seal (e.g., Texas has a star and Louisiana has a pelican).

The terms "partner" and "partnership" are frequently used inaccurately. The proper name for an owner of a corporation is "stockholder." A stockholder may also be a director, which is the name of a member of the governing board or body of the corporation. Corporations must have certain corporate officers, usually at least a president and a secretary-treasurer. These may or may not be stockholders and/or directors; if not stockholders, they are simply employees of the corporation.

In most cases the principals, as well as any others working for an incorporated practice, are employees, even if they are also stockholders and perhaps officers and directors. They receive income as employees from their salary and as stockholders from the profits of the corporation, in the form of dividends. A stockholder's personal tax planning can greatly influence the choices he must make about the balance between salary and dividend in his income. Again, these decisions should be made in consultation with an attorney and a tax specialist and the fact that tax law continuously changes should be kept in mind.

There are many variations in the titles given to principals and other professionals in architectural firms. Some relate to the operation of the firm as a business, others to its operation as an organization for doing the work. In the former category are "partner," "president," "chairman," and the like. Some practices have more than one type of partner, some being "senior" or "general" as distinguished from others who may be identified as "junior." In this case the junior partners might not participate in company profitsharing at the same rate as the senior partners, and their involvement in management may be similarly limited.

Another common title is "associate," a term with no legal meaning since the firm assigns its own definition. In some cases the associate shares in profits on the basis of a formula but does not participate in corporate management nor assume responsibility for financial or professional risk. This type of hierarchy is a way in which a long-established firm can share the fruits of an effective practice with deserving subordinates without relinquishing control of the firm.

In summary, the organizational structure of a firm is important not only in terms of the efficiency and quality of the work done and output produced but also in terms of its tax and professional liability and that of the individual principals.

11

Internal Office Management

The topics discussed in this chapter include, for the most part, tasks associated with administration and a few in other areas outside the direct scope of the design/production/contract-administration continuum.

PERSONNEL

The basic resource of an architectural office is people, what they know and what they can do. Managing personnel is a discipline about which scores of books have been written and in which one can receive graduate degrees. No attempt will be made here even to give an overview of the subject. However, a few points might be mentioned that can be helpful to the prospective employer.

In selecting technical personnel, the most obvious attribute to look for is technical competence. This is not always easy to judge. The applicant usually brings in some samples of his work and the interviewer asks him some questions about it to see if he really understands what he has produced. It is difficult to judge from drawing samples the speed with which they were produced. There is a direct relationship between a technician's speed and his value to the firm, a relationship that some, unfortunately, never realize.

1. OFFICE ADMINISTRATION

A. Corporate (Or Office) Planning
B. Personnel
C. Employment Applications
D. Equipment/Furnishings/Automobiles
E. Leasehold/Real Property
F. Insurance
G. Registration
H. Marketing
I. Photos/Slides

2. FINANCIAL MANAGEMENT

A. Banking
B. Taxes
C. Accounts Payable
D. Billings/Accounts Receivable
E. Bookkeeping/Accounting

3. GENERAL

A. Miscellaneous Correspondence
B. Contractor List
C. Consultant List
D. AIA/Professional Activities

11-1   General Filing System

Assessing an employee's attitudes toward his work and his commitment to the work of a firm ultimately entails a subjective judgment on the part of the employer. Sometimes this judgment is faulty and a decision to fire the employee must be made.

Early in the life of a firm policies must be established for such matters as holidays, vacations, office hours, breaks, telephone discipline, sick leave, and the like. At some point consideration will probably be given to employee group, health, and/or life insurance, perhaps partially or totally paid for by the firm. Some employers are now offering dental-insurance programs. The employer has to pay not only an employee's salary but half the total Social Security amount paid on his employee's behalf. The other half is withheld from the employee's check.

As soon as decisions on these questions have been made, they should be written down and distributed to all employees. This becomes the basis of an office manual, which no doubt will be revised and added to from time to time.

In addition, in most cases state or local law requires unemployment insurance, and there may be a state and/or local unemployment tax, based on the total wages paid over a period of time, such as a full year or a quarter. Expenses over and above direct salary of carrying an employee constitute the "burden" that must be calculated and planned before hiring a new employee or in evaluating payroll expenses for any purpose. Anyone who has ever drawn a paycheck knows how many items can be withheld, federal income tax, FICA (Social Security), insurance premiums, and the like. Unless one has actually functioned as an employer, one probably has little understanding of the other responsibilities, either in terms of additional money or of the administrative burden of handling the federal, state, and local records and forms.

ACCOUNTING

In the final evaluation of an employee's financial worth to the firm a few factors must be included. This calculation is necessary if time is the basis of billing. Not only must base salary be figured but also a factor for profit to the firm must be included. In addition, the hourly rate for billing purposes must be adjusted to reflect actual time worked after deducting vacations, holidays, and sick leave, which often total about a month in which no work is done. When all these adjustments have been made and additional expenses added, the total should be compared with the base salary. Frequently the total will amount to as much as one and one-third times the base salary.

The "billing rate" is the dollar amount charged to clients for work done on an hourly basis. It is usually arrived at by calculating not only the direct employee costs described above for all employees, but also other office expenses not directly attributable to individual employees, in other words the overhead (rent, utilities, clerical help, supplies, etc.), plus a percentage for profit. These are totaled and divided by the base-salary expense, and a "multiplier" is derived, usually two and one-half to three and one-half times total base salaries. This multiplier can then be used to determine billing rates for an individual employee. For example, suppose the multiplier turns out to be 2.63 and Smith's base salary is $5.25 per hour. His billing rate is then 2.63 times $5.25, or $13.81 per hour.

Obviously, a firm can set its billing rates as it chooses and is not obligated to show the client how they were derived. However, the calculations just described are useful if only to prove that the billing rates chosen were high enough to meet the financial objectives and needs of the firm.

Nontechnical personnel may be engaged in as great or perhaps a greater variety of tasks as are technical personnel. Or, in many cases, all personnel are engaged in as many nontechnical as technical tasks. The former are types of work that must be done by someone. They include typing and other clerical or stenographic work, bookkeeping, housekeeping, making prints, making deliveries, and running errands. In some firms keeping track of the technical literature alone requires a full-time librarian.

One way of looking at management is to consider it as a form of accounting. Accounting in the usually accepted sense applies only to money or to those assets that have a readily determined monetary value. Some of the same concepts used in financial accounting can be transferred to the nonmonetary assets or resources of a firm, which, as has been noted, are people and by extension the time they apply to a project. Accounting for nontechnical as well as technical man-hours ought to be just as critical as financial accounting.

COMPUTERIZATION

A growing number of tasks lend themselves to electronic automation. As computer hardware and software are improved and made less expensive, more and more work, especially nontechnical and support functions, will be performed with the assistance of some form of computerized equipment. Word processors can now replace several typists and improve efficiency by allowing thorough editing and proofreading prior to printing. This kind of equipment is especially useful in preparing specifications, for example. Other possible electronic-data-processing (EDP) applications include estimating, structural and mechanical design calculations, bookkeeping, and even drafting. All of these and more are available today, if not yet universally economical.

It is even theoretically possible that some time in the future all the data in a set of construction documents can be reduced to electronic impulses on magnetic tape or disc and transmitted over wires to terminals in the bidders' and material suppliers' offices, the codes authorities' offices, and the constructors' job-site offices. It might never be necessary to convert all the data to hard copy at any one time.

Wide-scale computerization will require somewhat different skills from those needed today, though the end product of an individual's labor ought to be unchanged; only the means of reaching that goal will be different. New skills will still require people. Management of personnel time and efficiency will be just as vital in the future as it is now.

We have not come close to investigating all the ways in which computer technology can be used in general office management, much less in architectural offices. One application that seems to offer high potential is in the area of personnel time management. As will be shown in a later chapter, effective project management is in large part dependent on effective management of the time the technical personnel put into a project. Using the computer to record and produce a periodic compilation of time charged to a project, along with the actual dollars this time represents, can help keep the internal budget for a project in line. It can also, if properly used, help keep a project on its calendar schedule. It is easy to envisage multitudes of applications, limited primarily by access to equipment, data banks, and programs and by the economic feasibility of employing them. As volume of use goes up, however, costs ought to come down.

MARKETING

Effective management of a firm's marketing and business-development efforts is just as essential as in any other line of work. A distinction is usually made between marketing and business development in that the former is more directly project- or market-oriented (see Chapter 9) and the latter is more concerned with general promotion of the firm's reputation to the public and the client groups toward which the firm's marketing plan is directed. For management purposes, at least, both can be considered part of the same basic effort.

This is an area in which effectiveness or efficiency is extremely difficult to judge on the short term. A person may spend months working diligently to create the climate for effective marketing to a particular client group and have no visible results until an avalanche of work appears. It is conventional wisdom that one contact out of ten will produce a lead and that one lead out of ten will turn into a real project. A huge amount of time, on average, has to be spent to produce one real project.

Clearly, effective use of time in marketing is essential. Most firms fail, however, because they are not able or willing to invest enough time early enough in the marketing and business-development plan, a prime example of the penny-wise-pound-foolish adage. What often happens is that a firm is so busy with current projects that it neglects marketing altogether until the work begins to run out, then anxiously begins a frantic scramble to stir up more projects. The development of new projects simply takes time, and the result in this case is a slack period and a consequent loss of income. Examination of past financial records can give insight into the kind of planning that will even out or avoid production peaks and valleys.

OFFICE SPACE

Pesonnel management also includes decisions and actions relating to the physical and psychological space and environment needed for effective work. Office design is an area each architect ought to be competent in without further assistance. Perhaps, however, some considerations ought to be mentioned that might otherwise be overlooked when one is both designer and client. It is possible to squeeze many people into a small space and at least on paper prove that they ought to be able to work, but it is much more likely that the difference between being able to work and being able to work effectively and efficiently will make the difference in the success or failure of the firm.

The work space must be large enough, sufficiently well equipped, and located appropriately in the work-flow pattern of the office. To say this to professionally trained designers may seem to be unnecessary if not insulting. However, when one also has to make decisions on how much and what kind of office space the firm can afford, compromises have to be made. It is easy to choose the financially expedient path over the initially more costly option that, in the long run, ought to be the more profitable. Such decisions, obviously, ought to be made on a sound financial basis, but the work space and its effect on such intangibles as staff morale and pride are an important part of the overall success of a firm. Taking a long-range view of decisions relating to the work space can help assure that success.

Another aspect of office space ought to be mentioned, the question of renting versus owning the space. Very few architectural practices can afford to set up initially in their own facilities. Not only is it unlikely to be financially possible but it is also difficult to predict what the firm's rate of growth will be. An office purchased before the nature of the practice has a chance to unfold will likely prove to be not only inadequate in size but also in physical arrangement.

One of the risks of building ownership is that, in order to provide room for the growth a firm desires and expects, it may be necessary to purchase or build more space than it can initially use. One answer to this is to rent out the surplus space until it is needed. This is not always easy to do but it is a possibility worth pursuing.

Nevertheless, for essentially the same reasons that home ownership is so attractive and beneficial, ownership of an office building or condominium will undoubtedly be one of the more important and beneficial long-range goals of an architectural practice, at least for its principals. Money previously going into someone else's pocket in the form of rent will be going into building equity for the principals.

If a firm is incorporated, a separate corporation should be established to own the property, which should then rent it to the professional corporation. In law this is referred to as an "arm's-length" relationship and it helps avoid entangling the finances of two essentially different business enterprises. In an unincorporated practice, these distinctions are less important.

12

Financial Management

The downfall of many a struggling architectural practice is undoubtedly the result of poor or nonexistent financial management. In order to survive, not to say thrive, it is necessary in any business to give constant and intense attention to financial matters.

It is necessary to know what money is coming in and what must go out and when. This is called "cash flow." It is essential to know how much money is required to operate—that is, to pay for personnel salaries, rent, utilities, telephone, supplies, and consultants. Other essential data include cash-in-hand, net worth, tax liability, and profit and loss. This information is essential for successful management of a design firm. For example, it is not possible to determine whether a new employee can be added to the staff on a profitable basis unless one knows beforehand the monthly or weekly minimum operating costs for the office, can judge the effect on this figure the additional personnel expense will have, and compare that to the anticipated additional income the prospective employee would produce.

The figure calculated from such an analysis would be the basis of salary negotiations. This means that an applicant may very well be worth more to one firm than another, but no factual estimate of his potential worth can be made without this kind of evaluation. Furthermore, the evaluation cannot be made without the appropriate records. This same process would apply in determining raises for current staff.

Comparing cash-in-hand to monthly operating expenses will show how many months the office can operate on current funds. In any business there is a potential of income cutoff for reasons beyond the control of the company. This seems to be more prevalent in design offices than in other types of business. Since the "products" in architecture are so large in comparison to most businesses, the financial health of a firm depends on single pieces, or projects. Likewise, in smaller firms where fewer individual projects are in progress at any one time, each project represents a larger share of the potential income compared to a large, diversified office. Consequently, if one major project "goes bad" and the future income it represents disappears, the result can be disastrous. For such reasons sound financial records and planning are essential.

It is easy to see the benefits of building up as large a cash reserve as possible, or a reserve in easily convertible assets. However, in certain forms of business, especially corporations, it is necessary to liquidate any reserve at the end of the fiscal year or be subject to heavy tax liability. Steps can be taken to avoid this sort of problem, but without adequate financial data as far in advance as possible they may not be possible.

Bookkeeping involves recording the daily transactions of the firm in several different formats for use in managing the firm. The simplest form of bookkeeping is the office checkbook, though by itself it is rarely adequate. Bookeeping functions, like engineering, can be performed either by in-house staff or by paid consultants.

An accountant, in the strict and commonly understood meaning of the term, analyzes the financial data produced by the bookkeeper, which is derived from the bookkeeper's records, and makes recommendations on taxes and other matters. An accountant or an accounting firm usually prepares the tax returns for the firm and, if requested, for the individual proprietors. It advises the firm on investments and on the financial component of many kinds of management decisions.

The difference between bookkeeping and accounting is that bookkeeping is essentially concerned with record keeping on a daily, weekly, monthly, and/or yearly basis, whereas accounting is concerned with analysis of financial records and future projections. They are like two complementary sides of the same coin. For reasons of impartiality, accounting is almost always handled by outside consultants rather than in-house staff.

REVENUE

The term "revenue" refers to all the money that is earned by the firm from whatever source. It is limited to money that is not only earned but also collected, since in any practice there will probably be a certain percentage of work for which total earned compensation is never received. This can occur for a number of reasons, the most prominent of which is that the client is a poor risk.

Very few architects go through their careers without having to resort to at least the threat of litigation to collect part or all of a fee. When a problem in collecting reaches this point it is fruitless to plan on receiving the full amount due. Lawyers will get a sizable portion, usually one-third, of any funds ultimately received if they are involved in the proceedings. Even if the client eventually pays all that is due, the architect will recover only a part of what he is owed.

The lesson in this is obvious: avoid situations in which collection is likely to be a problem. The difficulty lies in predicting when that will happen. Check the financial standing of any prospective client. Identify who in a corporate body has authority to obligate them to the agreement for services. Make sure that person concurs on the terms of the agreement, as one of the signatories if possible.

There is nothing unethical or unbusinesslike in requesting an advance payment, such as 20 percent of the fee on the first phase of the work. This act alone should screen out some financially marginal clients.

It is better to do nothing than to take a money-losing project. Some architects have been pressured in lean times to take a project on a losing or breakeven basis, because "it'll keep your people busy." It can also prevent them from being available for the next project, which may be profitable.

Every firm will lose money on some projects; one of the objectives of financial planning is to minimize this. The responsible practitioner never knowingly accepts a commission on a less than profitable basis, unless it is consciously done as a contribution to some

METHOD	FOR THE CLIENT		FOR THE ARCHITECT	
	ADVANTAGES	DISADVANTAGES	ADVANTAGES	DISADVANTAGES
PERCENTAGE	Easy to budget the project.	Automatically inflates cost; rewards architect for increases in construction cost.	Income generally well related to work required.	Penalizes architect for keeping construction cost down; open to question about what is included in construction cost.
DIRECT MULTIPLE OR COST PLUS	Pay only for what is requested.	Open-ended, not easy to predict final costs; no incentive to architect for efficiency.	Direct income/work relationship.	No opportunity for additional profit derived from internal efficiency.
PROFESSIONAL FEE PLUS EXPENSES	(Same as Direct Multiple/Cost Plus)	(Same as Direct Multiple/Cost Plus)	Minimum profit level is assured.	(Same as Direct Multiple/Cost Plus)
FIXED SUM	Easy to budget the project; opportunity to negotiate for exact services required; built-in incentive to architect for efficiency.	May be difficult to accept Architect's basis of fee calculation if the Client has never done it this way before; the idea of a large sum of money may be harder to accept than a percentage.	Charges based on estimates of work required; opportunity for profit derived from internal efficiency; allows more precise production planning.	Difficult to determine at beginning of certain types of projects.

12-1   Comparison of Various Compensation Methods

nonprofit enterprise. The successful firm does not indulge in many such contributions.

Revenue is produced by the work produced, the services performed. For such work payment as specified by the owner-architect agreement is due. The most frequently used formats for such agreements are the AIA documents described in Chapter 8. They allow the parties to choose one of several possible methods of determining compensation. The most common are the following.

PERCENTAGE OF CONSTRUCTION COST

This is the traditional method that for decades was almost universally used by the profession. The total basic compensation (less specified expenses and extras) is derived from a percentage of the construction cost of the project. There might be different percentages for different types of work, such as remodeling versus new construction and work let to a single general contractor versus work let directly to multiple subcontractors. It is easy to see that these variations can be a fair way of compensating the architect for the extra time put in for a similar construction cost in differing job conditions. It is likewise easy to see that sorting out what percentage applies to what part of the job can be anything but easy. An acceptable definition of "construction cost" can sometimes create problems, as when the owner furnishes some of the labor and/or material directly to and for the project.

DIRECT MULTIPLE OF EXPENSE OR COST PLUS

This is a method in which the time of the technical staff is computed and billed to the owner at the billing rates discussed in Chapter 11. In addition, certain other agreed-upon expenses are billed to the owner, including the consultant engineer's bills, often at a multiple of 110 to 125 percent. The questionable feature of this method is that it is open-ended, unless limited by the terms of the agreement to a maximum amount.

PROFESSIONAL FEE PLUS EXPENSES

This is a variation of the cost-plus method, with a fixed-sum professional fee added to the other expenses. The professional fee would seem to represent the profit the firm would expect to receive for the project, and fairness would indicate that a somewhat lower multiple of payroll expense would be used, since in the cost-plus method profit must be included in the hourly billing rates. This, too, is an open-ended method unless a maximum amount is named in the agreement.

FIXED OR LUMP SUM

In this method a fixed sum for basic services (less specified expenses and extras) is negotiated before work begins. Care must be taken to accurately assess the time and expenses required to do the work. This can be difficult to do in many cases, since the scope of the project is not very tightly defined until after the preliminary design has at least started. However, it does offer, when properly utilized, the highest potential for profit; it rewards the firm for its own efficiency. Furthermore, it gives the owner a firm amount to budget for architectural services for the project.

There are variations and combinations of these methods and others used in certain sectors of the economy. For example, some developers of shopping centers and other retail work like to use a method that bases the compensation on so many cents (or dollars) per square foot in the building. A popular combination is to use the cost-plus method for the preliminary design or until the scope of the project can be set, and then to convert to a fixed sum for the remaining phases.

In almost all the methods the usual practice is to exclude certain expenses from the basic compensation plan and include them as direct pass-through charges, perhaps with a multiplier. Examples are costs of document reproduction, long-distance telephone calls, telegrams, travel, and lodging.

The standard agreement forms also exclude certain items from the basic services and identify them as additional services or extras for which additional charges will be assessed if performed. These are at the owner's option and include models, professional renderings, photographs, interior-design services, detailed cost estimates, and a number of specialized tasks not usually considered part of the typical project. (A more thorough discussion of the different methods of determining compensation can be found in *Profit Planning in Architectural Practice* and *Compensation Management Guidelines for*

Architectural Services, both published by the AIA. The latter takes a somewhat different approach, being directed toward profit goals rather than to any specific compensation plan, although it lends itself more readily to the fixed-sum method.)

There are many considerations in choosing which compensation method to use. Each has advantages and disadvantages, both for the owner and for the architect. Some clients, such as some state and local governmental agencies, are required by law to use one of the methods, usually percentage of construction cost. Until the Department of Justice labeled them illegal a few years ago, standard fee schedules were published by some professional groups, such as local or state AIA components. Some of these schedules were on a sliding scale; the lower the construction cost, the higher the percentage used in computing the fee. (In the mid-1960s the Tennessee Society of Architects successfully lobbied for a sliding fee scale to be used on all state projects. It is based on the formula:

$$\text{fee} = \% \text{ of construction cost} = \frac{35}{\log \text{ of construction cost}}.)$$

The national AIA claims that it has never published a mandatory or even a recommended schedule.

A fee can be any amount, based on any method, that the two parties to a professional-services agreement have agreed on. What is important for the architect is to make sure that it is adequate for the work to which it relates.

PLANNING

Earlier discussions have stressed the importance of a constant work flow. Money is the fuel that keeps an office operating and a constant work flow means a constant flow of money. In every kind of business long-range planning is desirable. In architecture it is not as easy as in product-related businesses, for the same reasons mentioned in Chapter 9 in the discussion on marketing. This is true because the level of activity in an architectural firm is more subject to external factors and other parties than to the principals and other personnel of the firm. Nevertheless, advance planning ought to be attempted to the degree feasible.

One direction it can take is strictly financial: to determine the personal income the principal or principals wish to receive during the next planning period, usually a year, and then project from that the financial activity that would have to occur for the specific personal incomes to be produced. This type of calculation, sometimes called a "profit plan," can be made without great difficulty. (Though somewhat dated in specific dollar amounts, the procedures shown in the AIA booklet *Profit Planning in Architectural Practice* are excellent for this purpose.)

Going through such an exercise in no way guarantees success. It does, however, identify what has to be done if the goals are to be met. It also can be of great assistance in evaluating the effects of hiring new people, laying off others, or giving raises, and in identifying necessary marketing objectives.

In the sole proprietorship, profit translates directly to personal income. In most instances in practices of this type the principal takes a periodic "draw," similar to a salary but actually an advance on future profit or a withdrawal of profit already earned. At the end of the fiscal year a determination is made of the difference between income and total expense. Any overage is profit; a negative figure is a loss. If a loss occurs, the principal may have to reimburse the firm account for the excess drawn. This amounts to adding capital to the enterprise without any corresponding increase in worth; in this case it is an expedient emergency action and not an action that promotes growth or any other improvement in the business.

In other types of business structures similar conditions may exist and must be guarded against. Spotting losses early is difficult but necessary to avoid serious financial trouble. For this reason it is usually good practice to have the bookkeeper prepare monthly, quarterly, and annual profit-and-loss statements.

A thorough understanding of capital, what it is and what it is not, is essential. Capital is the money that must be provided initially to equip a firm for practice, whether it is borrowed or brought to the practice by the principal. It corresponds to and actually is investment money. It is not a fund to be used for ongoing or operating expenses; these must be met by current revenues. Capital is increased in the same way that any investment is increased, by return on investment or profit. It may be reinvested in the form of new equipment or furnishings, but it is still carried on the books and therefore represents an increase in capital for the owner of the business or the principal.

When asked to name their most important goals of practice, most architects probably would not name profit. However, any architect who wishes to remain in private practice very long has to recognize the crucial place profit has in permitting him to realize the goals he would name. Profit is possible because revenue or income exceeds expense, the prospect of which can be greatly enhanced by diligent and careful financial planning.

13

Office Management
By Project

This chapter deals with general and supportive tasks and procedures that relate to specific projects but do not involve actual design or production.

First, it would be helpful to define the term "project." For the purposes of this discussion a project is any specific assignment, the culmination of which is expected to be either a completed building or a long-range plan or other research effort resulting in a more or less formal report.

It is usually, but need not be, work for which the firm expects to be paid. Almost all offices occasionally do gratis work for worthy causes or small favors for friends for which no remuneration is expected. The question arises, however, in how to keep track of the time spent on this kind of effort. Even if no income is expected, it is still good management to account for time actually expended. The best procedure is to formally identify each job as a project. In most offices this involves assigning it a number—a project number, file number, or job number.

One recent book on financial management for design offices questions the necessity and usefulness of project numbers. While on the surface this may seem to be a reasonable idea, long practice will show that the advantages of using project numbers to keep track of time, files, and everything else relating to individual projects far outweigh the disadvantages. For example, one of the hallmarks of a successful practice is repeat business from the same clients. Repeated use of the client's name for project filing could cause great confusion and complicate the retrieval process. On the other hand, assigning a number to each individual project makes record keeping and retrieval much simpler with no added inconvenience. Once a project-number system is set up, if it is adequate in scope, it will be self-policing.

FILING

Files are set up and time is recorded on the time sheets for each job. The project number system can be assigned on any method of the principal's devising; but, since numbers of at least three and, more often, four digits are involved, they can be put to use in management. Using part of the number to identify the calendar year in which the project began makes it easy to keep project files in chronological order. Sim-

PROJECT NO.	CODE	TITLE/CONTENTS
0000	– A	OWNER CORRESPONDENCE/To and from the owner
0000	– B	BILLING/Professional services agreement, invoices, statements
0000	– C	BIDS/Bid forms, bonds, subcontractor lists, bid tabulations
0000	– D	CONTRACTOR CORRESPONDENCE/To and from the contractor and subcontractors on the project
0000	– E	CONSULTANT CORRESPONDENCE/To and from engineers and other consultants
0000	– F	CONTRACTOR PAYMENTS/Construction contract, applications for payment
0000	– G	CHANGE ORDERS/Copies of change orders at all stages
0000	– H	SUBMITTAL LOG/Log of shop drawings, catalog cuts, samples, etc.
0000	– I	SUBMITTALS/Shop drawings, catalog cuts, etc., that can fit into a file
0000	– J	MISCELLANEOUS CORRESPONDENCE/General or unclassified correspondence

13-1   Project Correspondence Filing System

ple alphabetical order is not as useful, since it lacks the more or less automatic feature of culling outdated or inactive files of a chronological system. Again, many projects have complicated names that are not easily locatable in an alphabetical system.

Files should be structured but flexible. A small project that is not anticipated to take much time may need only a single folder. Most projects probably require several, and a uniform filing system, one in which the same kind of information is found in the same place in each set of files, is needed. Any system can be chosen, as long as it is consistent and flexible enough to accommodate the demands of the largest project.

Without a doubt, government work generates the most paperwork, not only that prepared and sent to the government, but also correspondence and other records received by the design office. For the paperwork of even a moderate-sized government project, an entire standard file drawer may be required. The higher the level of government, the more the paperwork. Keeping track of it is even more essen-

SECTION	CONTENTS
GENERAL	Minutes of owner-architect meetings; instructions from the owner; telephone memos, etc.
PROGRAM	A brief program statement, modified as necessary to reflect latest information and decisions; important owner constraints such as budget and deadlines; applicable code information, etc.
PRODUCTION	Schedules for the entire project span from schematics through occupancy; office budget; working-drawing-sheet schedule and manhour allotments.
COST DATA	Restatement of owner's budget; all estimating calculations; building-area computations; comparative costs of alternative assemblies, etc.
TECHNICAL DATA	Worksheets on such items as stairway dimensions, window and door sizes, sketch details; spec sheets of equipment; exit calculations for code conformance; photos of existing conditions, etc.

13–2   Project Notebook Organization

tial than for private clients for the simple reason that it is government work.

In addition to the correspondence files, many offices maintain a system of notebooks in which design and production notes, memos, work sheets, key personnel names and telephone numbers, minutes of client meetings, area calculations, code summaries, technical data, and the like are kept. They may be passed from the design team to the production team in an office organized on the horizontal model (see Chapter 10) and, along with approved preliminary drawings and outline specifications, become part of the design package that governs the production of the construction documents.

In addition, the drawings produced must be kept in a filing system keyed to the project by the same project number used for all other documentation. Flat files are used most frequently for active projects. There are several methods available of handling inactive files. Fiberboard flat files are probably sufficient as long as they are not subjected to frequent stress. Tube storage systems come in several sizes, types, and levels of quality. If room is available, bins can be constructed in which rolls of project drawings can be stored. The essential measures of acceptability of any system, however, are the ease with which any specific project may be found and retrieved and the protection it affords the documents.

One storage method that will no doubt become more common in the future is to microfilm the drawings and specifications. The cost of having work microfilmed has gone down dramatically since it was first introduced commercially, and it may soon be cheaper than adequate storage containers, not to mention the cost of the space they take. In the future even more advanced methods of storing and retrieving graphic material such as architectural drawings will undoubtedly be developed. Instead of microfilm they might be copied on magnetic tape by some sort of high-resolution videotape system, for example. One potential advantage of electronic technology is its rapid retrieval capability.

However, two reservations to these high-technology developments can be raised. One, much of what an architect produces during the design process and wishes to keep is not what finally appears on the construction drawings or even the final presentation drawings. Many times sketches are done on scraps of flimsy or memo-pad sheets that would be difficult to fit into a highly structured system. Two, the level of output of the typical design office is not likely to be large enough to justify the expense of such sophisticated machinery for a long time to come.

PROJECT MANAGEMENT

Varying in position and formal title with the office, some one individual must be directly responsible for the project at each stage of its progress through design, production, and construction. As was noted in Chapter 10, in an office organized on a horizontal basis the project is passed on to a different manager or supervisor at each level of work. In a vertical organization, the same individual probably stays with the project all the way through, at least until construction begins. This person may be called a project architect, a project manager, a principal, a partner-in-charge, or any other formal title. Different supervisors or managers may be responsible for different phases under the overall supervision of the permanent project architect or manager. The larger the project, of course, the more levels of management are likely to be needed, and new titles may have to be devised to denote the division as well as the level of responsibility.

In many small- to medium-sized offices, especially in sole proprietorships, a pattern has evolved that seems to work rather well as long as the temperaments of the parties involved complement each other. In this pattern the principal has one or more employees who function as executive assistants for particular projects. This assistant will be responsible for all the detail of the project, while the principal will maintain whatever degree of oversight is needed. In this way the principal can delegate responsibility and authority and extend control to several projects at one time. As much or as little of the design activity as wished can be delegated in this way, depending also on the capabilities of the individual project assistant and the principal's personal interest in the project.

Another frequently found pattern in sole-proprietorship firms larger than the very smallest is for the principal to isolate himself from the daily detail of project activity through a single assistant, who then relates to individual project managers in a similar way to that just described. The principal in this case may spend the bulk of his time on one or two tasks, such as marketing or design. In a partnership one partner might concentrate on marketing or administration or both, while a different partner devotes his time primarily to design, as has been discussed in a previous chapter. This structure can also function with the single executive assistant described above.

There is another pattern, which is frequently described in writings about architectural practice but which is actually very rare, for the simple reason that it doesn't work for very long. In this pattern a group of individual principals, say three to six, get together and decide to pool resources—manpower, space, equipment, and the like—in order to cut down expenses and become more competitive for larger projects. The idea is to draw from a common manpower pool, including themselves if available, as individual projects require. They can go after a larger project together or pursue their own markets.

This sounds very good on paper, but the trouble with this type of practice is the common fault of "too many chiefs"—planning can become too uncertain, rivalries can emerge, and disputes over the commonly held resources can arise. There may be a few practices of this sort around the country, but the majority are probably transitory in nature; that is, the people involved in them are on their way to another, more stable environment.

In the more formally structured multipartner firm, a project-management form similar to the loose affiliation just described may exist and function effectively. In such a firm each of several partners would have a project-management structure similar to one or the other of the two forms first discussed above.

14

The Project Processes

This chapter discusses in somewhat deeper detail the activities relating to individual project management. The several phases of the typical professional-services agreement are covered, beginning with the agreement itself.

THE SERVICES AGREEMENT

The different types of compensation plans, as well as several other aspects of a services agreement, were discussed in Chapter 12. However, most such agreements and certainly all using the AIA document forms structure the work into certain formal phases and define the relationships and the responsibilities of the signatory parties in certain standard ways. With few exceptions these are the same no matter what the compensation plan may be.

The owner, unless otherwise stipulated, has to furnish to the architect a complete site survey and, if required, a sub-surface-soil-investigation report. This information must be available before the design, at least a detailed version, can be completed. The owner should also provide a budget or a statement that there is no limit (though this will probably never occur within an architect's lifetime). In reality, thre are times when the owner is flexible about the amount of money available for the project; there are also times when the budget cannot be determined with any great certainty until the architect has at least done the basic research and begun the preliminary design.

It may seem obvious to say that a services agreement must be made before work on the project can begin. The truth, however, is that in many cases, because of an architect's eagerness to please and to get on with the project, work does start before an agreement is formalized.

Recalling the discussion on profit in Chapter 12, it is easy to see that by beginning a project without an agreement the architect may be throwing away some of his negotiating power on issues that can mean the difference between a profitable and a losing endeavor. Even if time dictates that work begin before a formal agreement can be prepared and signed, it is always best to reach an understanding with the owner on all key points, make him aware of the architect's intentions, and give him the opportunity to react.

It should be remembered that the standard agreement form is a document with which the architect is very familiar, since he has probably used it in essentially the same form several dozens of times in just a few years. The owner, on the other hand, may not have had any previous contact with any form of this type; the project may be his first and only one. Therefore, great care should be taken to make sure that he understands everything about the agreement and approves of it.

PROGRAM

Few owners understand what an architect means by the term ''program'' unless the architect explains it. The same could be said of many other terms used in services agreements.

There are two reasons for calling attention to the program at this point; one is that it is usually excluded from the basic services in the agreement and is therefore an additional service; the other is that, even if no provision is made for a formal space program in the agreement, either in basic services or as an extra, the information and decisions frequently formalized in a program must be provided if a meaningful design effort is to ensue. It may be as simple as ''four bedrooms, three baths, den, two-car garage, and the usual other stuff.'' Nevertheless, the owner's needs must be identified in some way; and, if the project is large and complex enough, the program should be handled in a more formal manner.

The program should perhaps be viewed as only one of what might be called predesign activities. Others might include market research for projects planned for later resale, real-estate feasibility analyses, or site evaluation. Programming, however, is probably the only predesign activity that is apt to be necessary on almost every project.

DRAWINGS AS COMMUNICATION

In the orthodox scheme of architectural projects there are three phases in which the principal medium is the drawing, with some involvement of the written word and perhaps a model.

One and possibly the most important way of viewing these drawings is as communication. In the schematic-design and design-development phases, that communication is with the owner. It is a two-way communication; the owner is telling the architect what he wants, and the architect shows in his presentation drawings how he interprets those wants and how he has translated them into a proposed building. The owner responds by reacting to the presented design and, through dialogue, revisions are made until both parties agree on what will be done in the schematic-design phase and on the more specific decisions in the design-development phase. Schematic design is for basic concepts; design development is for refinement.

Design development is also communication with the construction industry in general and, if a project is to be negotiated, perhaps with a specific constructor in particular. The decisions an owner makes in this phase must be informed decisions. This may require information from building-industry sources; in order to give valid information, these sources probably need drawings.

The drawings in the construction-documents phase are communication with the builder or builders. The type of information they need is quite different from that of the owner. They need to know how to build the building. These drawings are truly the "blueprints" for putting together the building (even though almost no one uses real blueprints anymore). The contractor is not really concerned with how the building will look or what kind and quality of human activity will take place in it. A sensitive builder, and there are many, actually cares and cares deeply, but what is on the drawings that he uses in the construction does not address those feelings. Their purpose is to make it as easy as possible for those who are going to work on the building to understand what is to be built and how. This is the communication content the drawings should carry.

SCHEMATIC DESIGN PHASE

While the documents (drawings, reports, models, etc.) produced in this phase may be voluminous, only a very small percentage of them are usually seen by the owner. He sees the finished work, what the architect wants him to see after all the head-scratching and doodles have been done, all the reasonable options for design solutions generated, evaluated, and chosen from. For this reason it may appear from the owner's point of view that the work produced in this phase is disproportionate to the fee compared with later phases. However, the architect not only needs to understand but also communicate to the owner that the time spent in this early conceptualization period could very well be the most important in the entire project. Those hours and the work accomplished in them set the course for all work that follows. If adequate time is not devoted at this point, the project may be doomed to some degree of failure, if not in serious deficiency in the usefulness of the completed building at least (or at best) in a mediocre building.

This phase is not limited to design, but also to other material developed and presented in it to the owner for approval, such as an outline specification and an estimate of costs. This means that time must be spent to ensure that the estimate especially is adequate and will remain so during the evolution of the project. It is not only embarrassing but may also wreck the project for the owner to be told at each succeeding phase that the budget must be increased, unless a very good reason can be cited, such as an increase in its scope. It is good practice to provide in estimates prepared during this phase healthy allowances for items not yet fully identified.

The real purpose of the schematic design phase, of course, is to identify in graphic form the scope of the project, the relationships of various elements, the general form or forms of the building, and its visual character. When this has been done competently and adequately and has been accepted by the owner, it becomes the map, the set of guidelines, the instructions for the development of the project in later phases. It becomes a yardstick with which to measure the work of the later phases. The program may have assigned square footages to both individual rooms and entire buildings, but not until the schematic design phase will it be known whether the assumptions made and factors applied in programming can be transformed into a real building, nor can its character and quality be established.

WEST ELEVATION • PRELIMINARY DESIGN STUDY • 12/8/80

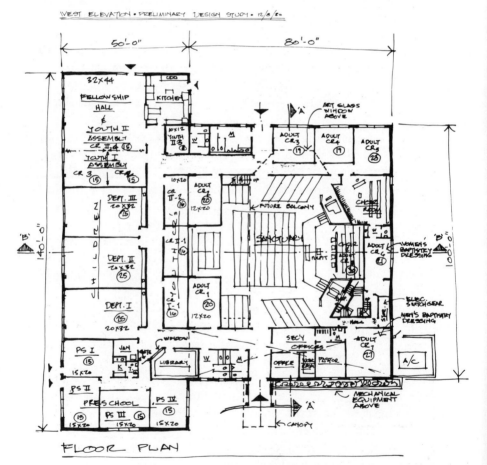

FLOOR PLAN

14–1A   Schematic Design Phase Sample Drawings

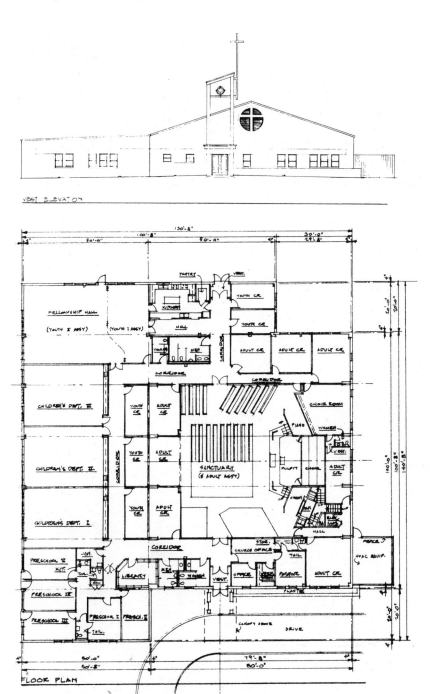

14–1B   Design Development Phase Sample Drawings

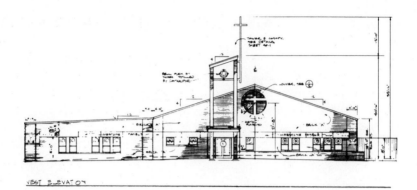

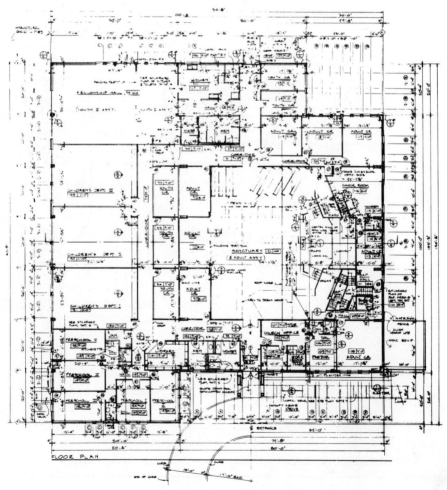

14-1C   Construction Documents Phase Sample Drawings

DESIGN DEVELOPMENT PHASE

This is a transitional phase between the schematic design and construction documents phases. While the drawings produced in the schematic design phase are, of necessity and by definition, somewhat loose and flexible, the design development documents are intended to "tighten up" this looseness and begin to nail down particulars.

Drawings in this phase usually are made at a larger scale, frequently the same scale at which the working drawings are drawn; problem areas too small to be seen at the schematic design level begin to become visible. Such details as door swings are shown, which invariably result in a few adjustments. At the schematic design level it is easy for the designer to deceive himself about critical dimensions in tight quarters; at the design development level these discrepancies should become apparent and their solutions can then be worked out.

In the design development phase the basic layouts of the engineering systems should be determined. These may or may not appear on the drawings presented to the owner for approval at this phase, but it is necessary to have the information available in order to integrate into the drawings that are presented the governing parameters the engineering systems apply to the design. This is especially critical for structural design. The design development drawings show overall key internal dimensions, and the designer needs to be certain of their "fit" with the structural system.

The design development phase also includes upgraded outline specifications and cost estimates. Under the provisions of the standard AIA agreement forms, the cost estimate at neither this phase nor the next (construction documents) need be a detailed, quantity-takeoff type. Amendments to the agreement, however, can require such an estimate at either or both phases.

While the axiom "the earlier, the better" can and should be applied to the task of code review, as a practical matter preliminary review by code officials, if available at all, is often meaningful and ultimately useful only if done at this phase and no earlier. This is true for the same reasons that were noted above about door swings, tight clearances, and such; schematic design drawings are usually too rough to allow much credence for critical code issues.

At any rate, whether done in-house, by private consultants, or with code officials, this phase is the proper point to "prove" and nail down the assumptions about code requirements made earlier. If adjustments in design need to be made due to code requirements, this is the time to make them. If serious questions arise, which may indicate a challenge or lead to a request for code relief or other variance, it is better to halt the design and production work at this stage until the question is resolved rather than to proceed and hope for a favorable ruling. If this were not the outcome, the additional time and expense might be lost with no hope of recovery.

The purpose of the design development phase is to settle all the issues noted above and others of similar nature. When these have been settled to the satisfaction of the owner and others involved, such as code officials, then the project is ready, the "decks are cleared," for the next phase.

CONSTRUCTION DOCUMENTS PHASE

This phase, the most time-consuming of the three design-production phases, may be the easiest to describe and understand. It is simply the production of the working drawings and specifications plus other documents necessary for bidding (if this is to be done) and construction. The complexity of this work depends on the complexity of the proposed building project. It can vary from a single drawing sheet on which all pertinent specifications are included to several hundred drawing sheets and several volumes of specifications.

This phase may sometimes seem less glamorous than the earlier design phases, but it is certainly no less important. Furthermore, as it represents an actual building that must meet codes, satisfy the owner's needs and expectations, and be buildable in detail not required of the two prior phases, it exposes the architect to a much higher level of liability and other kinds of risk. In other words, in authorizing the production of the construction documents the owner is legally committing the team to a real construction project. Had the project been terminated at one of the earlier phases, no liability for its soundness would fall on the architect, since it would not become a real building. Professional-liability-insurance premiums should reflect this in that the fees earned, which are used in determining premiums, should be divided into those earned on projects that progressed or are expected to progress to real buildings and those that did not.

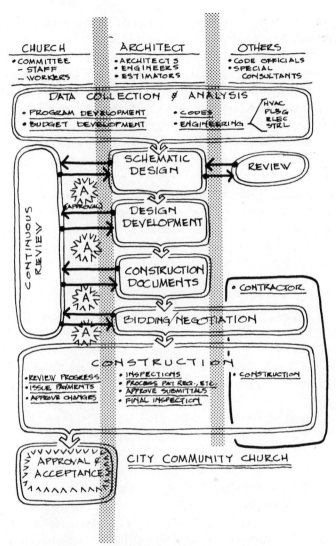

14-2   Sample Phase Work Flow Diagram

Naturally, every conscientious architect is going to be aware of his ultimate responsibility at every stage of a project. The point here is that it is only if a building is actually constructed that certain important aspects of this responsibility become real, and they begin to become so at an accelerated pace in the construction documents phase.

One difference between this phase and the last may be made clear by assigning the tasks of data gathering and research to the design development phase and their technical application to the construction documents phase. This is especially true regarding materials, products, and equipment to be used in the project. The manufacturers of these items literally flood design offices with catalogs, samples, and brochures. The storage and handling they require can be a real burden, and the wise office manager will plan for the space and manpower to deal with them adequately.

In addition to the ubiquitous Sweets' catalogs (collections of product manufacturers' literature, organized into the Construction Specifications Institute's sixteen-part format and bound in several large volumes, published by McGraw-Hill), many manufacturers provide individual catalogs of their own line, many larger and heftier than any single Sweets' volume. The most helpful manufacturers also have available on call technical representatives, either on the manufacturer's own payroll or in the employ of a distributor or wholesaler of their product, who can discuss with the designer the best use of their product or the best product for a particular application. Some representatives must be sought out; many, however, make themselves well known to the architects and call on them frequently, bringing new product literature and updating catalogs and samples.

The basic investigation of products for possible use in a project and for tentative selection should begin in the design development phase. However, in the construction documents phase it is necessary to make final selections and to do so with the assurance that they will actually do what is expected of them.

It has been pointed out earlier that since one of the key resources available to a design office is its manpower, the "accounting" of that manpower is just as important as financial accounting. In the production of drawings this can be aided by carefully assigning and monitoring personnel time applied to the drawings. One way in which this may be done is to assign a target number of man-hours to each planned sheet and each day enter the hours actually spent on that sheet into a log. The log is often kept right on the tracing itself, sometimes on a clipped-on tag or a transparent stick-on at the extreme left-hand edge (under the binding when the drawings are printed and bound).

Computing the target numbers is not an easy task but it can be done with practice and experience. If the total compensation is

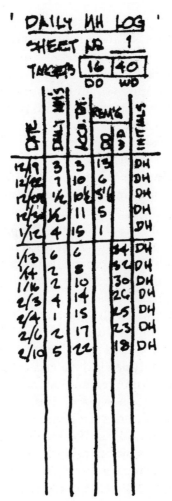

14-3   Manhour Target and Log

known or can be estimated, then progressive reductions from that amount, accounting for work in other phases, work by consultants, and factors for overhead and profit, yield a dollar amount available for actual drawing time. This will be less than the total money available for the construction documents phase; it will even be less than the total available for production, since experience shows that only a part, perhaps only half, of the man-hours spent in this phase are spent directly on the drawings; the remainder are spent in checking, consultation, and coordination. When a final figure is determined, it is then converted into man-hours, based on a historical average for this kind of work and distributed and assigned per sheet. The analysis and assignment may include the design development phase as well, since the same tracings are often used for both phases. (Another planning aid is a sheet-planning form in which boxes are provided for sketching in the work planned for each sheet, much like a TV or movie storyboard. Accuracy is promoted by using a transferable scale: sketches drawn at 1"-100' compare to drawings at a scale of 1/8" = 1'-0" on a 24" × 36" drawing sheet; 1" = 50' compares to drawings at 1/4" = 1'-0". It is not perfect but it can be useful in avoiding both self-deception as to how much can be included on one drawing and the production of too many sheets. This form is shown in Appendix 2.)

Chapter 8 included an explanation of the project manual, which consists not only of specifications but also of instructions to bidders (if required), a work summary, general requirements, and the general and supplementary conditions. Some offices have experimented by including in the project manual certain standard details drawn on an 8½ × 11-inch page. However, it is better for the workers in the field to have all details on the drawing sheets; bound sets of the project manual may not be distributed as widely as drawings. (As a general practice, it would probably be ideal if all specifications also appeared on the drawings for the same reason. In practicality, the more specifications that can be put on the drawings, the better, even if they repeat what appears in the project manual.)

If the project is to be bid, the construction documents must include bidding instructions, part of the project manual. If the project is to be negotiated, this section is not included, of course, but other provisions might have to be included in their stead. In many if not most negotiated projects the actual negotiation will have begun during the construction documents phase or even earlier, when the input of the negotiating contractor can be applied most usefully. The detailing and material selection can be tailored explicitly to that contractor's unique capabilities. In a project to be bid, these choices have to be sufficiently open to allow all bidders an equal advantage.

Another critical task of the construction documents phase is coordinating the work of engineers and other consultants into the whole and with each of the other specialties. A very close relationship exists between the electrical and mechanical disciplines, for example. The space taken by ductwork and piping designed by the mechanical engineer must meet space tolerances governed in large part by the structural design. The architect is responsible for the whole design and is the only design team member who is. This phase is his last opportunity to see that it fits together in the best possible way before the design is presented to the world for execution, use, and evaluation.

DOCUMENT PROTECTION

Article 8 of the AIA Standard Form of Agreement (Document B141) is entitled "Ownership and Use of Documents." This article clearly establishes the fact that the ownership of the documents remains with the architect and that the drawings and other documents produced for a client are "instruments of service." The owner is not paying for the drawings, although elsewhere the agreement provides that the owner will receive at least two "copies" of all documents issued in the course of the project. He is paying for the service that the drawings have been produced to provide.

In spite of this protection, there have been cases when unscrupulous owners have tried, and occasionally succeeded, to reuse the drawings on a different project without paying the architect. In addition, other parties have sometimes obtained a set of drawings and attempted to use them without paying for their use.

The disservice to the architect is twofold. First, it is patently unfair. Second, it exposes the architect to risks occurring in the unauthorized project for which he has received no compensation and over which he has no control. He may not even be aware that it has happened until he receives a summons to court in the case of a worker injured on that project. Stranger things have happened.

In order to further safeguard drawings (drawings are what really require protection; the specifications are useless unless applied to a specific project), the architect can either copyright each drawing or place on it words establishing its ownership and that it cannot be used without express permission of the architect. The first is probably more legally supportable; the second easier and in practice probably more effective. Our office places on every working drawing and on many schematic design drawings as well words similar to these: "This drawing and the design shown is the property of XYZ Architects. The reproduction, copy, or use of this drawing without written consent is prohibited and any infringement will be subject to legal action."

One important application of this kind of protection at the schematic-design phase is in the case of a development-site plan produced for zoning approval. This kind of drawing, for Planned Unit Developments and other large-scale, multibuilding projects, is often produced for a developer who only has an option on the land. If he decides not to proceed, some other developer may at a later date pick up the architect's plan and proceed with the development, leaving the architect out of the project altogether. Attaching a warning paragraph similar to that above may prevent this from happening.

There is, of course, no sure-fire, totally secure way to protect one's drawings and designs from unauthorized use. Diligently using the kind of device described here will probably give as high a degree of protection as is possible to have.

BIDDING OR NEGOTIATION PHASE

Whether a project is to be bid or negotiated, the objective of this phase is to secure for the owner a contract or contracts for the construction of his building project.

For simplicity the discussion here is limited to a single-contract project. Multiple-contract projects can take many forms and may be even more prevalent in the future than today. However, for the size of project likely to be the norm for small practices, the single-contract project will probably remain much more common.

The process of negotiation, or at least its beginning, was mentioned under the previous heading. Its culmination will be the same as if the project were bid. When a satisfactory proposal from the contractor has been received by the owner, a formal contract can be drafted, signed by owner and contractor, and work can begin.

The bidding process is somewhat more complex, formalized, and time-consuming. In addition to the construction documents, the architect must prepare the bidding documents. These include instructions to bidders, which tell what and where the project is; who the owner and architect are; when and where the bids are to be received; allowances, retainage terms, and the amount (percentage) of bid bond (bid bond is a form of insurance policy guaranteeing that the bidder will sign a contract for the work at the amount bid; the bond is usually in an amount of 5 percent of the bid sum, which is forfeited to the owner should the bidder refuse to sign such a contract if offered) or other security if required; performance-bond description if required; where to obtain bidding documents; the bid or plans; deposit amount if any, and any other pertinent information.

The information mentioned above is often published in a public-notice advertisement in the local newspaper, especially if it is a government project. In addition, on government work it is usual public policy to allow any licensed contractor to bid on a project. Many locales have offices of F. W. Dodge Corporation, which publishes for its subscribers lists of projects coming up for bid. The subscribers are for the most part contractors, subcontractors, and material suppliers. In major cities there are often one or more local contractors' associations, which will provide parallel services. These offices, including Dodge, also provide "plans rooms" where the actual drawings and specifications for projects in the bidding period are on display for their subscribers. The Dodge firm also lists projects not yet ready for bidding and those being negotiated.

If the project is for a private or nongovernmental owner, it may be thought best to limit the bidders to a select, prequalified few. Candidates can be submitted by the architect; the owner may have some he wishes to include. The architect's responsibility is to screen the qualifications of those being considered and recommend a proposed-bidders' list to the owner. It is the owner's task to make a final decision. The contact with the possible bidders may actually begin before construction documents are completed, with steps taken to find out if they are interested, capable (especially in terms of bonding capacity), and will have the manpower and material available at the time the project will be in construction. The financial history and strength of the bidders should be determined. All this information might best be recorded on some kind of standard form, which will make comparisons easier. A typical form is shown in Appendix 2. The AIA also publishes a bidder qualification form (AIA Document A305).

In addition to the above, the architect must include in the documents issued to bidders a bid form (see Appendix 2). Not only must it provide blanks for the dollar amounts of the base bid and any alternates but also such information as the length of time anticipated for completing the project and unit prices for items not specifiable in advance. Unit prices are usually used for earth or rock removal but can also be used for any other item on which the owner wishes to reserve decision until later in the project.

A word about base bid and alternates may be helpful. A frequently used technique when there is uncertainty about cost and about the owner's available funds is to bid certain parts of the work as alternates. There are two basic types of alternates—deductive and additive. In a deductive alternate the amount bid for the alternate is to be deducted from the base bid; in the additive alternate this bid sum is to be added to the base bid if the alternate is taken or accepted. Experience has shown that the owner usually receives a better dollar value on additive alternates. The base bid is, of course, the sum bid for all work not covered by alternates or unit prices.

A period of time is provided, varying in length with the size and complexity of the project, during which the bidders prepare their bids. The bidders must receive prices from their subcontractors and suppliers, some of which are taken as competitive bids, which in part explains the need for the time. In most cases for projects of up to several million dollars in size, the bidding period is usually around four to six weeks. During the bid period questions that require an answer, a clarification, or a decision are received from the bidders. Sometimes these questions point to a conflict in the documents that must be resolved. Rather than respond to each question individually, the architect should receive them without verbal comment and issue a bulletin or addendum to all bidders at the same time. (Many offices do not distinguish between these items, or use "addendum" exclusively. However, "bulletin" can be used for those responses before a construction contract is signed, and "addendum" for those occurring after or at the time of such signing. This difference is based on the rationale that afterward any such action is an addendum to the contract, while before it is simply new information.)

A frequent and useful practice is to have a prebid conference involving all bidders. Sometimes this is done at the beginning of the bid period but it may be more useful around the midpoint, since by then the bidders will have had time to review the documents and raise any questions. A multi-item bulletin may be one result of such a conference. If the project is a remodeling or an addition, the prebid conference may be conducted at the site.

Another practice sometimes used to reduce printing costs and for convenience is to have the construction drawings reduced to one-half size (dimensionally) and issued to bidders, with a cover letter explaining the scale reduction. If carefully drawn, these reduced prints should be sufficient for bidding. When the actual construction begins, full-sized drawings are issued.

On the appointed date and time and at the appointed place, the bidders turn in their bids. The bids are usually in a sealed envelope, which contains not only the completed bid form but also any required bonds and perhaps a completed bidder-qualification form. Another frequently requested item, often submitted in a separately sealed envelope, is a list of proposed subcontractors. In some states the contractor's license number is required to be on the outside of the exterior envelope.

In government work, a designated governmental official usually officiates at the bid opening; in private work the architect usually presides. A frequent courtesy is to provide for all bidders, the owner, and anyone else present a blank form on which to record the bids as they are opened and read. The official record may be made on the same form (see Appendix 2).

At the actual opening each bid envelope is taken in turn (alphabetically if no other order is indicated). Before opening the envelope, the bidder's name is read aloud and the envelope is examined for external conformance with bidding requirements and law. This too is announced aloud, as are all other readings from the bids. Then the envelope is opened; determination is made (and announced) whether all required items have been included (bonds, subcontractor list, etc.); and the bid form is read. Often it is only necessary to read the entire bid form on the first bid. On subsequent bids the appropriate words and figures may be read.

This may conclude the formal meeting. The bidders should be thanked for their participation and an announcement made as to when a decision may be expected and perhaps arrangements for return of bid deposits. If a clear low bid is received and it is within the owner's budget, that bidder may be asked to remain to discuss further details about the forthcoming work.

If all bids are above the owner's budget, several options are available. If one bid is clearly close, a decision might be made to attempt to negotiate with the low bidder. If this is not the case, the project may be abandoned; redesigned and rebid or negotiated with a single contractor; or simply rebid at some more favorable later time. None of these is an attractive prospect for either the owner or the architect. It tells the owner that the architect has not done his job properly, even when there might be conditions outside the architect's control that contributed to the situation, some of which may have been caused by the owner's own decisions, lack of communication with the architect, or self-deception. At any rate, it is at best an awkward situation for the architect and one from which he must extricate himself as graciously as possible, while protecting the interests of the owner to his fullest ability.

When any and all questions have been resolved and the owner is ready to sign a contract, the architect usually prepares it and distributes it for signatures, most often to the contractor first. He also requests from the contractor the initial items specified by the construction documents—performance bond (if required), progress schedule, and other submittals. At the owner's instruction, the architect issues to the contractor a notice to proceed, which marks the official date for commencement of construction.

PRINTING AND BID DEPOSITS

One of the common practices of architectural offices over the years has been to maintain a link between the bid deposit and the cost of printing the drawings and specifications. The reason was that for a long time these costs were expected to be included in the basic fee the architect charged.

Sometime within the last couple of decades, someone at AIA must have read his doctor's bill in detail, seen all the lab and other extra charges tacked on, and said, "Aha! what a great idea to adapt to architectural service agreements." The standard form of agreement sprouted a shopping list of "reimbursable expenses" and it now includes reproduction costs. This means that the owner pays for these costs directly, or with a small multiple for handling.

The old practice was to estimate the costs of printing and make that figure the bid deposit. The deposit of the low bidder was kept by the architect in order to recover the printing expenses. However, when the agreements began to require that the owner pay the printing costs, many firms, out of habit more than intent, continued the practice of basing the bid deposit on the printing costs and of keeping the bid deposit. This meant that the owner was paying twice for the printing; no doubt the bidder was including the deposit in his bid, since by winning the bid he would be forfeiting the deposit. It also meant that the architect was being paid twice. It was not only unfair to the owner but it also inflated the cost of his project.

The purpose of the bid deposit is to give the bidder a financial incentive to submit a bid if he takes a set of bid documents. It is of no benefit for the owner to go to the expense of putting a set of documents into the hands of a bidder only to have the bidder decide afterward not to act on it. A secondary purpose is to provide a mechanism for limiting access to the plans; that is, to make it less likely for sets of an architect's plans to be floating around the offices of unsuccessful bidders. These might be picked up and carried off by anyone and in the wrong hands might be used in some building project that the architect has no connection with. It has happened.

The proper way to handle the bid deposit is to set the deposit at some level that will serve the purposes described above and to return it to the low bidder as well as to the unsuccessful bidders. Our practice is to return the deposit only if the documents are returned "in good condition" within five days after the bid opening. We also allow bidders and subcontractors to purchase second sets at a reduced cost and refund a major portion of that charge upon their return.

Some firms make it a practice not to issue partial sets or single sheets to bidders or to anyone prior to the execution of a construction contract. On one particular occasion a structural-steel subcontractor got hold of a print of a single sheet issued during the bid period, which was later revised. He began to use this unrevised print in the fabrication of the steel. Some dimensions had been changed in the revisions and were not caught in the shop-drawing review (remember, the architect is not responsible for checking dimensions). It is easy to see what happened—some steel of incorrect length was shipped to the job and had to be returned and refabricated. It slowed the job down and cost someone a lot of money. The contractor tried to recover from the architect but finally agreed to absorb the cost. Nonetheless, much ill will was generated, which from that time on could and has been avoided, at least from this particular source.

Printing in-house has become a legitimate profit center for many firms. If space and manpower at the right cost are available, running prints in-house and charging the client rates comparable with commercial printers can be a profitable enterprise. It will not produce great amounts of money, but it will produce some that the firm would not otherwise receive.

Two cautions, though. One, mentioned above—don't let greed cause you to act unfairly toward the client. Two, in some states sales taxes may have to be paid on printing done in this way.

CONTRACT ADMINISTRATION PHASE

Some of the steps described in the last paragraph above more sensibly belong in this phase. Whatever occurs after the signing of the construction contract and the notice to proceed is part of contract administration. In this phase the architect engages in three primary activities—job observations (or inspections), pay-request processing, and submittal processing.

The initial job-site visit may be a formal preconstruction conference, at which all questions can be brought up and worked through.

The frequency of subsequent visits depends on the nature and size of the project, as well as on the weather and speed of the work.

Each month (usually) the contractor submits to the architect his application for payment. The most frequent form used is AIA Document G702 with G702A. On it will be listed in dollars, by trade and for subcontract, the work accomplished during the pay period, the work accomplished prior to the period, and totals less retainage, arriving at a total amount requested for the period. The architect's task is to examine each item and satisfy himself that the supporting claims of work accomplished are accurate and that the total is fair and reasonable. If it is, he signs the form and forwards it to the owner for payment.

The accuracy of the various items may be difficult to determine except as a subjective judgment. Occasionally an error is obvious, such as when money is claimed for materials that have not been delivered to the job site. Some items may have to be referred to the consultant engineers for verification. If adjustments have to be made, the architect makes them on the application form before he signs the form and sends it on.

All this must be done quickly because the contract usually contains a schedule for processing the pay requests. The typical requirement is that, if the contractor submits the request by the first day of the month, the owner is obligated to pay him by the seventh or eighth day of the month. This allows the contractor to pay his bills by the tenth; some of his suppliers will give him a discount for payment by that time and, especially if the project has been bid, he has counted on these discounts in preparing his bid and in agreeing to the contract sum.

Another activity parallel to processing pay requests is monitoring actual progress as compared with the progress schedule submitted by the contractor. If the progress lags, through this device it may be spotted early enough to make correction relatively easy to accomplish. It also can act as a mechanism to alert the parties that the cumulative claims for work accomplished, as shown on the pay requests, may be running beyond the pace of that shown on the progress schedule.

On large and complex jobs and on those in which there is an extremely critical completion date, the progress schedule may be a CPM (critical-path method) chart or similar computer-assisted device. Usually, though, a simple bar chart suffices, with parallel spaces for

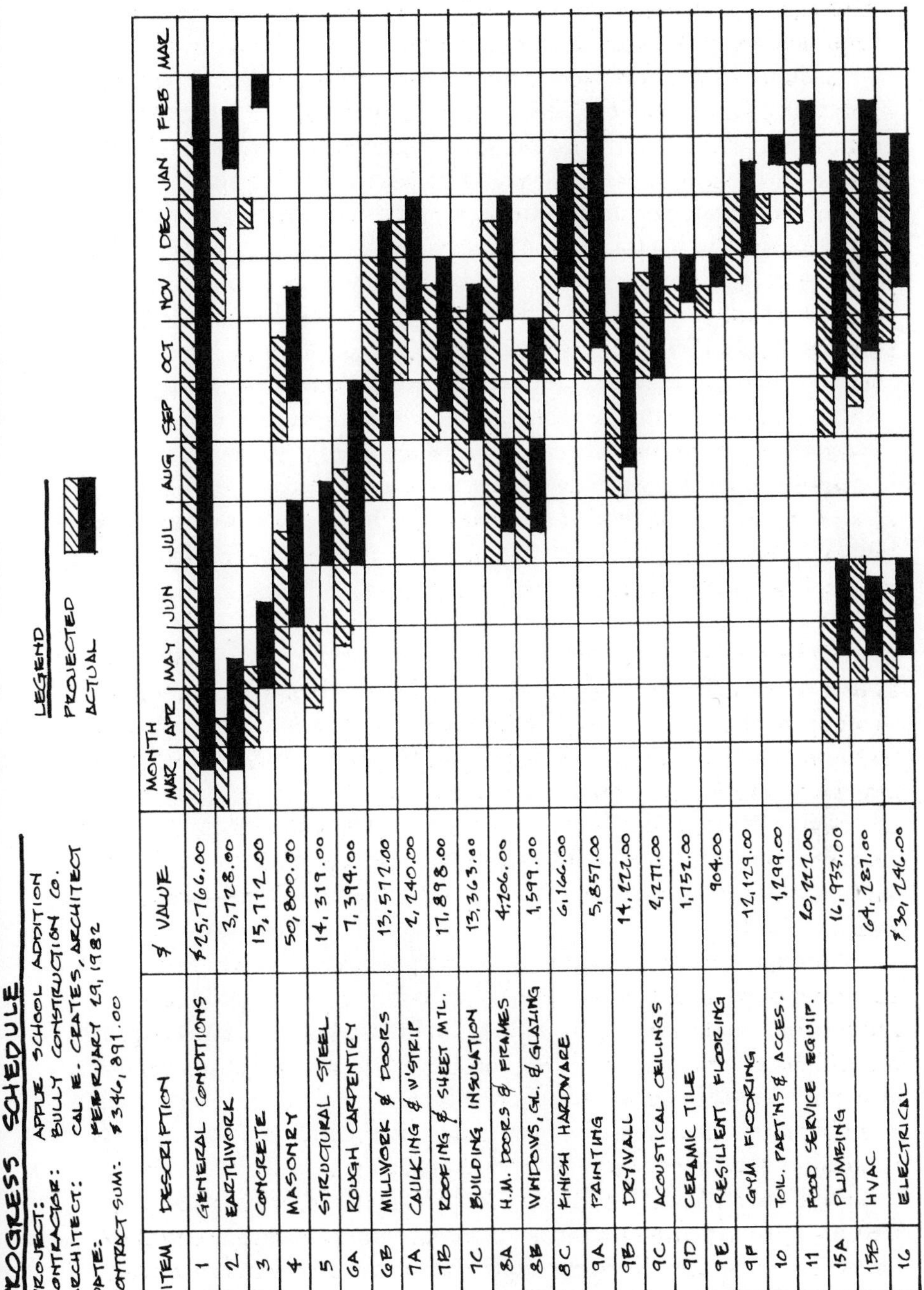

14-4 Progress Schedule

"projected" and "actual" work allotted for each trade division and subdivision along a calendar base.

"Submittals" is a term covering a large body of items that the contractor is required by contract to submit and receive approval for before proceeding with the project. These fall into three categories—shop drawings, manufacturer's literature, and physical samples.

Physical samples are for the most part items of finish such as floor covering, resilient base, ceiling tile, wall coverings, ceramic tile, roofing, brick, paneling, wood moldings, and the like; or manufactured goods that are concealed in the construction, such as rigid insulation used for roof decking. The reason for submitting these is that in most cases similar products can be obtained from several manufacturers. It is seldom to the owner's advantage to have an absolutely closed specification, with one and only one product acceptable. Accepting similar products from other manufacturers provides an element of price competition that should reduce the cost. The checking of submittals ensures that the substituted product is in fact equal in every critical way to what was specified.

The same rationale applies to manufacturer's literature (sometimes referred to as catalog "cuts") and shop drawings. Literature often accompanies samples and shop drawings as part of a submittal for an individual item. Some submittals are collected by the subcontractor into groups such as plumbing fixtures, HVAC equipment, HVAC controls, lighting fixtures, and the like.

When submittals are received, they are entered into a master list or "log," which is a record of what has been received and when, its status, and the final action taken on it. Submittals are usually given a number for ease in tracking. Some submittals have to be forwarded to the appropriate consultant engineer for checking, and the log shows forwarding and return dates. A sample shop-drawing log is included in Appendix 2. Also in Appendix 2 is a combination shop-drawing transmittal letter and log, which was developed for a joint venture project in which our office was a partner.

Shop drawings are frequently blue-line prints and in part often duplicate details shown on the architect's drawings. The term "shop" refers to the supplier's shop where the items are actually made. The purpose of shop drawings is twofold: to give the architect an opportunity to see that the item will be made up as intended and to give the manufacturing workers a drawing that shows only what they are to produce and one which has been drawn in the format and with the standards with which they are most familiar.

The shop-drawing process is critical. In a building project, which is a one-of-a-kind product, there is no opportunity for prototype construction and testing to "get the bugs out," as there is in industrial manufacturing. The shop drawing is one means of partially compensating for this lack. It creates the opportunity, for example, to show that a very minor change, which may seem inconsequential to the supplier, may make it impossible for this item to fit with another furnished by a different supplier. Checking shop drawings from both suppliers ought to make it possible to spot this kind of discrepancy and to make the required revisions.

Occasionally the submittal is judged so deficient that it has to be rejected and resubmitted. When checking shop drawings and other printed submittals (such as the hardware list) the architect usually uses a red pencil for its attention-getting quality. His final action is noted by approval, approval-as-revised, or rejection and is usually shown with a rubber stamp in which the action is noted, with the date and the checker's initials. Care must be taken in the wording of the approval stamp to avoid including more than the architect intended. He should exclude, for example, approval of dimensions, since the contractor has overall responsibility for dimensions and any item fit-

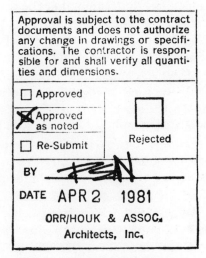

14-5   Shop Drawing Stamp

ting into the whole must be fashioned to fit the conditions *as they have been built,* not necessarily as the architect designed them.

The description in Chapter 9 of the project closeout is sufficient as a summary. In frequent cases, the process seems to take forever, with the owner holding back until every possible contingency has been resolved. The contract, specifically the general and supplementary conditions, includes safeguards to protect the owner after closeout. These are the guarantee-warranty provisions. Despite this, some owners are loath to trust their ability to get a contractor or subcontractor to return after closeout, and justifiably so in many instances, and thus want everything exactly right before final payment has been made.

A key provision in the general conditions is the Date of Substantial Completion, defined as the date on which the owner could occupy and use the building, even if all work has not been completed. It is also frequently the date, especially if the facility is actually occupied at this point, marking the commencement of the guarantee-warranty periods. It is the architect's responsibility to decide the date of substantial completion. Its critical nature can readily be seen and the care with which the architect exercises this responsibility cannot be overemphasized.

The usual scenario for project closeout is for the contractor to notify the architect and owner that the project is ready for final inspection. The inspection is scheduled to include the consultant engineers where appropriate. From it will be produced a list of deficiencies or a "punch list," which is given to the contractor, who then proceeds to correct the deficiencies. The engineers may produce their own punch lists. If the list is sufficiently long, it may be decided that the project is not in fact ready for the final inspection. Some architects have included in the supplementary conditions a provision for additional compensation for the time and other expenses of a "false start," or being called to a final inspection when the project is not yet ready.

If the list is of reasonable length and the items are relatively minor, it may be decided to declare that date the date of substantial completion and authorize payment of the remaining contract sum, less the retainage. When the items on the punch list have been worked off, the remainder of the retainage is then released for payment.

In most construction contracts a percentage of earned monies due the contractor is held back to cover possible undiscovered deficiencies. This is known as the ''retainage'' and the most frequent figure is 10 percent. In some locales an emerging practice is that, after the project is 50 percent complete, no further retainage is withheld. The result is that each month thereafter the retainage reduces as a percentage of work is accomplished until at the time of closeout it totals 5 percent.

An amount greater than the retainage may be held from the final payment if the work remaining is judged to be higher in value and cost than the retainage amount.

Each project has its own unique story. The smoothness or lack thereof in the operation of the various tasks and relationships depends in large part on how well the architect has done his job in preparing for construction, but perhaps even more so on the personalities of the parties involved, the human factor, which cannot be avoided. Learning how to deal with it is just as essential in architecture as in any other field.

15

Other Services

Architects are frequently called on to perform services other than orthodox building design. These may be adjunct services, such as interior design or graphic design. They may be part of a larger design problem, such as site master planning or urban design; or they may be more or less unrelated to a particular building project.

ENERGY

One topic about which every architect as well as everyone else is going to have to learn more in the coming years is energy. In addition to learning more about designing energy-efficient or energy-conscious buildings, architects may be called upon to evaluate the energy efficiency of existing buildings—to perform energy audits, in other words. A logical and expected outgrowth of this is the design of energy-efficient retrofitting measures. It would be hard to guess how many books have been written and published on energy, how many manufacturers of solar collectors and other energy-saving devices have sprung up, and how many energy "experts" have appeared just in the few years since the 1973–74 oil embargo; no doubt hundreds or even thousands in each category. There is also no doubt that a shakeout is now underway in which the survivors will be those with real assets to offer to the public. There is no reason why architects should not be at the forefront in energy consultation. It may not be for every architect or every firm, but energy is a growth industry and some architects will by temperament and personal interest be well advised to direct their practices toward a specialty of energy consultation.

REAL ESTATE ANALYSIS

Another area in which some architects have been active, either as a service for clients or for their own business, is real-estate-feasibility analysis. This is a technique of evaluating the economic prospects of a proposed commercial development involving construction before any design is done. Developers do or have this done for them on every project under consideration; it is what is meant by "running it through the numbers" or some similar phrase.

With the passing from the scene of the fixed-rate mortgage and low interest rates this process has become more difficult and less certain. Moreover, the day of land development to the extent at which it existed when this process was developed may have passed. However, there will probably always be some form of land development or redevelopment, at least as long as there is a free-enterprise economy, and architects should be open to possible participation in it. They can offer a cluster of services including design and financial analysis or participate in the development itself, as some notable examples have shown in the past. In fact, building or purchasing one's own office is a form of development, and many of the decisions and arrangements involved in that activity are also found in more conventional land development for speculation and investment.

INTERIOR DESIGN

Of the adjunct design activities available to the architect, interior design is probably the most prevalent. In the broadest sense, it is simply a logical extension of architectural design. In reality, however, the business climate and features of interior design are quite distinct from traditional and orthodox architectural practice. The chief difference is that for many years the only way the service was available was on the basis of commissions on sales of products—furnishings, wall coverings, fabrics, and accessories—and subcontracts such as for painting. This is still the way much of the business is conducted, especially in the residential field.

In recent years a form of service not dissimilar to architectural service has emerged for what is known as the "contract" field—large-volume commercial interiors. However, even though offered as a consultant service—writing specifications, doing furniture layouts, and the like—for a fee, many of the sources are also dealers of furniture lines and other interior products. The contract-interiors industry is attempting to resolve this dichotomy and to introduce as much professionalism as possible into the field. Many large architectural offices now have interior-design departments, which operate purely as a consultant service in the same manner as their parent architectural firms operate. In terms of dollar volume, however, the sales-based firms probably still account for a healthy majority of the percentage.

Interior design is not a field in which a small architectural firm can occasionally dabble. It must be an established and well-funded department or staff function. There is no other way to compete. This means that within architectural firms involved in interior design there are personnel who devote their full time to this area of work; they become specialists in interior design. It certainly can be a worthy activity; and, if the opportunity appears to be good and the interests of the architect lie in that direction, there is no reason not to become involved in it.

Even small architectural firms can offer interior design to their clients, in the same way as they offer the services of their engineering consultants; that is, under a consultancy subcontract with an interior-design firm. The availability of such a firm may be limited or nonexistent in some locales.

MASTER PLANNING

Master planning is an inexact field of work, inexact in that the term has no well-defined, precise, uniformly accepted meaning. It can be as little or as much as the architect and his client want to make it. Master planning is frequently employed when the client is an institution with a large plot of land that it intends to develop and expand into over a span of years. Examples are churches relocating to a new site, colleges, and office-park developments. Many of the techniques of urban or city planning are brought to bear and reports of considerable depth are produced. These techniques include population analysis or

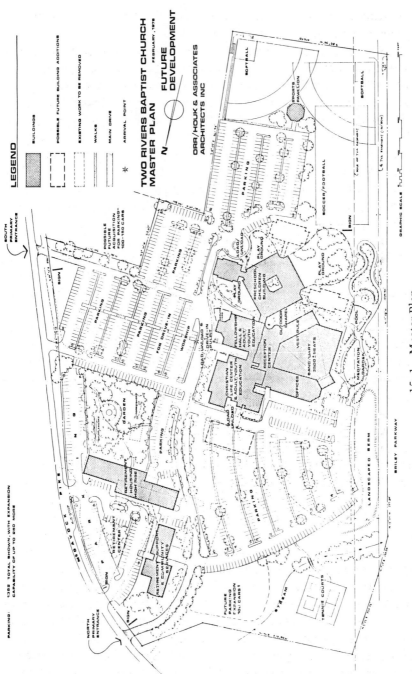

15-1   Master Plan

demographics, potential adjacent development and its impact, future public-works projects in the geographic vicinity, and growth in other urban factors such as airline travel or school population, which would all affect the proposed development.

As done by architects, master planning usually includes at least an analysis of the geographic features of the site proper—slopes, natural shading, wind, access roads, and the like—and recommendations on placement of future building increments as well as supporting facilities such as parking. As office projects they are often coupled with the initial design phase of a proposed building. Indeed, on a virgin site it may not be possible to do a thoroughly professional job of designing the building without also doing a minimum-level master plan.

Urban-design projects are similar but may not lead to the design of a building. Instead, the design, in the traditional sense, may be for a fountain, a plaza, or other ''space between'' buildings in an urban setting.

Such a project may run into the field of landscape architecture. Many multidisciplinary design firms include landscape architecture as a service. The field of landscape architecture is not recognized everywhere as a profession in the same sense that architecture is, due to the fact that not all states require licensing, and many people offering the services are, like some interior designers, primarily in the business of selling products, in this case plants. This is not to say that there are not many talented and perfectly ''ethical'' (professional) landscape-architecture firms. The field is so loosely defined, however, that there is no reason why architects should not expand into it if they are capable and so inclined. Even in those states where landscape architecture is a legally recognized, registered profession, it is generally understood that registered architects can provide any landscape architecture service.

This discussion is not intended to be exhaustive; only the most common auxiliary services that architects sometimes perform are listed. Given the kind of broad-based, creative education architects receive, it is certain that other activities will be discovered by restless and inventive architects in the future. Also, as has always been the case, the future has a way of revealing its own needs to us and of creating openings for the alert to enter in meeting those needs. And architects ought, by training and temperament, to be more alert to these opportunities than most other people.

16

Future Trends

Almost everyone is a visionary. Architects, being in the business of envisioning buildings that do not exist and that hopefully will come to exist, are perhaps as well qualified as any to engage in the seer's game. It is not only an entertaining pastime but also a useful one, in that by seeing the future we can better judge present actions for their effect on future fortunes. The projections mentioned here are not at all original. Most have been expressed elsewhere by more qualified observers. They are included because of their potential effect on the subject matter of this book.

OFFICE SIZE

In the Introduction it was stated that this book's intended audience is those architects who wish to practice in small firms, but there seems to be a clear trend toward larger, multioffice firms. This is not to say that the small office will disappear. It may mean that, because of the economics of the construction industry, the medium-sized office will become more rare. The economic forces attending architectural practice seem to be driving it into one of two divergent directions—very large or very small. The small end would likely specialize in some area, such as historic preservation, remodeling, interiors, residential, retail-store design, or simply by size of project, and it would be located where there was sufficient work of that size to sustain it.

The projects now handled by medium-sized firms would, if this trend progressed to its logical conclusion, no doubt go to the larger firms. These superlarge firms would have within them small, semiautonomous project teams to which such projects would be assigned.

The superfirms may grow by accretion as well as by internal addition; that is, they may buy up and/or merge with smaller firms, often as a means of opening a branch office in a new location. The better-managed of these will offer architects much opportunity for personal and corporate growth and satisfaction, along with the security and the freedom from individual responsibility for the entire operation that falls on the private practitioner-principal. This may be the only way for the profession to survive the onslaught of nonregistered usurpers in the building-design arena.

However—all may not be quite lost. A few years ago when the population-explosion doomsayers were forecasting horrifying scenarios for the planet if the rate of population growth remained unchanged, some very wise person calmly pointed out that those dire results were patently impossible. Before the population could grow to the point, for example, where there was only one square foot of habitable land for each person, the forces of nature or acts of man or both would prevent it. As we have seen, the threat has somewhat lessened in that at least in the developed nations the rate of population growth has declined and in some cases nearly reversed itself.

If anything is certain, it is change and one type of change that is just as certain is that it is cyclical. No doubt the growth of the super-firm will be checked at some point, simply because laws of economics we may not be aware of today, or that may not be in effect today, will force such a change. ''The more things change, the more they stay the same'' may not be original but it is appropriate to recall when looking at the future. So is ''There is always room at the top.'' If an aspiring architect sees his most satisfying role to be in a diminishing vocational model, who can say that he cannot make it work for him? Who can say with certainty that the small firm is doomed to narrow specialization or second-class work for ever? No one.

In his excellent book, *Managing Architectural and Engineering Practice*, Weld Coxe talks about ''passages'' of architectural firms, the stages they go through over time. His examples are not universal nor inclusive. If they survive long enough, all firms go through several phases over the life of the practice. Some may be planned; some may "just happen." The wise practitioner will use these passages to further his personal and professional goals. Much can be done to shape a firm into the model the principals wish it to be with wise planning and the willingness to act when the opportune moment appears.

PRODUCT DELIVERY

In Chapter 5, the phenomenon of design-build was discussed. Again, because of economic realities and to a lesser degree greater public expectations for a single source of responsibility and faster delivery, design-build may become more common. This does not in all cases mean that architects are excluded from participating in the process. Many perfectly acceptable buildings have been designed by architects under contract to constructor-developers and other design-build contractors. In some small firms this type of work has become a mainstay. Probably it will never be the principal method; too many people are committed to the notion that competitive bidding is best, especially in public work and other projects for institutional clients. However, for private developers it, in all its variant forms, could become the norm.

Many owners will also be the builders of projects, and the problems of being only one-third of a two-against-one combine will challenge architects but should not defeat the better ones. One significant difference in the technical side of practice is that, in this kind of arrangement, much less detailing and specification is often required. The owner/builder wants as little on the drawings as he can get by with at the building department (he also has to pay less for it); he wants the greatest amount of freedom in making as-you-go, on-site decisions. The architect's liability could be affected in such cases, but careful wording of professional-service agreements can provide the required protection. As with design-build, there are many small firms that derive a majority of their income from such work.

The fast-track idea will probably grow slowly, as experience with it increases. The size and nature of projects to which this method is best suited will become clearer and the construction decision makers who wish to capitalize on its promises of speed and economy will know with more certainty the type of work in which these promises are most likely to be fulfilled.

Fast tracking is usually associated with construction management. In the future this may not be as true as it is today. Some small firms will be able to structure projects that require completion within extremely close time limits in such ways as to meet these limits. Some aspects of fast tracking as it is known today will be used, but other techniques will be invented. Architects have always been innovators. This characteristic will not change.

RELATIONSHIPS WITH GOVERNMENT

With the return of the conservative ethic in government one would be tempted to think that the tide would soon turn toward less regulation. This may be true in some fields but in the area of building design, construction, and use it may not be true at all. In fact, there will probably be continual tightening of building and fire codes, especially in light of several recent catastrophic fires and building collapses.

However, there may be some relief in governmental regulation of the business aspects of architectural practice. There may be tax relief and relief from record-keeping burdens. It may even become easier for small firms to gain access to federal projects.

On balance, architects will probably experience a net increase in governmental involvement in their work. It should be remembered, however, that most of this involvement is at least arguably beneficial to society at large.

ENERGY

So much has been written on this topic that the ennui almost outweighs the urgency. Nonetheless, energy considerations will become more and more important in both the design and the construction of buildings and in a firm's business decisions. Those who look for salvation in new oil fields, synfuels, gasahol, and hydrogen or electric automobiles are doing society a disservice by encouraging people to postpone due consideration of fundamental changes in lifestyle (which need not be any less fulfilling within the constraints of reasonable energy use). A reasonable prediction might be that western civilization will try many of these alternatives before rejecting the automobile as the primary means of transportation. The challenge is not to use up too much nonrenewable energy in the process, not to run out of what we need before we reach the point of no longer needing it.

The effects of the real and perceived energy shortages have already shown up both in design and practice. Energy-conscious building design in the future will not be a specialty field for a few but a basic, required skill of *all* architects; the definition of architecture will include "energy-consciousness," along with "commodity, firmness, and delight."

ELECTRONIC ASSISTANCE

This revolutionary tool will affect architecture no less than any other field. Its mushrooming applications are now occurring in two directions. One is the expanding availability and diversity of programs and access to them through remote terminals. This means that a firm of almost any size can have access to the most sophisticated computer assistance available, which the owner will pay for. It will make it possible for smaller firms to compete with large firms (perhaps contradicting what was said earlier in this chapter).

The other direction is miniaturization. Microsystems, now available at prices as low as several hundred dollars, are affordable for even the smallest firms and can be easily put to use in many business-management tasks. Experience will reveal more and more applications, from payroll to marketing to design.

CONTINUING EDUCATION AND PROFESSIONAL GROWTH

Society is sending the architectural profession conflicting signals. With some states tightening up registration requirements and the National Council of Architectural Registration Boards making graduation from an accredited school of architecture mandatory for certification on one side and with states such as California threatening to abolish registration altogether and failed candidates challenging the validity of registration tests in court on the other, what can be determined? What does society want of the profession?

It probably will continue to demand more accountability, for one thing. Despite the second two examples cited above, the drive toward tighter registration controls will probably continue and be the norm in most jurisdictions. For this reason, not to mention the perfectly valid personal reasons of professional improvement, continuing education will remain a growth field. Some states now require evidence of continuing education for continuing registration; other states are considering it. No doubt in the future the NCARB will require it for continuing certification.

In addition, professional growth and a professional attitude demand it. In the not too distant past the growth of information in architecture was relatively slow; the economy, even in times of war, was relatively stable and emerging viewpoints in the profession could easily be absorbed by reading the journals and listening to the technical representatives when they came by. No more! The knowledge explosion and uncertain times have made it imperative for every architect to continue his education in more direct and intense ways than in the past. He must consider his education never completed and must strive, even when not forced to by registration requirements, to achieve an appropriate balance, to always be a "complete" architect.

17

Summary and Recapitulation

In order to understand how to function professionally as an architect—as a businessperson as well as a designer of beautiful, useful, and sound buildings—it is necessary to know the worlds in which that profession lives. This means the economic and the governmental worlds as well as the cultural and social worlds.

There are many people playing many parts in these worlds. Some have certain congruities of interest with architects; some have few, if any; none has a perfect match of interests. Each sees these worlds from his own unique perspective.

Some people respond to the opportunity to participate in a project with an architect by maintaining an attitude of competitiveness—one-upmanship, if you will. They see commerce as a game to be played for high stakes, with definite winners and losers. They do not intend to be losers, and all their actions are governed by this world view. While such people are probably in the minority, it is wise to be watchful of them and to protect oneself as much as possible. The opposite, fortunately, is to be found in even more people; that is, a spirit of cooperation and helpfulness. They hold a world view that allows all parties in a transaction to be winners.

In his practice the architect must decide where his loyalties lie and remain true to them, even when temptation is high to compromise for expediency's sake; there *will be* many temptations. The architect must strike a balance between protecting the interests of his client, society as a whole, and his own self-interest.

No one on this earth can be totally altruistic. An architect who looks after the interests of his clients and society to the neglect of his own will soon be out of business and without a means to provide the services he is capable of and which his clients and society need. He must continually strive for internal efficiency in his office, for maximum effectiveness in his service, and for a reasonable return on the investment of capital and hard work he has put into the practice. He must recognize that it is in the client's short-term interest to pay the architect as little as possible. This is in direct conflict with the architect's self-interest. In addition, it sometimes is in the client's perceived interest to avoid spending money for some code-required provisions, which are there to protect the public health, safety, and welfare. This is another conflict of interest between the architect's two primary constituencies.

It may be that challenging apparently unreasonable code requirements is appropriate. Codes are constantly being revised and part of the input into these revisions results from official challenges. Not all challenges are capricious or in some way supported by a majority vote; some have merit and call attention to inequities that the code drafters did not foresee, or that over time evolved due to changes in circumstances.

Advice to the architect initially embarking on his own practice would include the warning that he will be faced with a much greater number of decisions and decisions with much greater consequences than he has ever imagined; he ought to gird himself with the most strength, wisdom, and integrity he can muster in order to deal with them.

While architectural practice is a business, while much of this book has been addressed to business aspects of practice, and while many business-management techniques and principles can and should be used, it should not be forgotten or ignored that people do not go into architecture primarily to make money. The motivations impelling architects to do what they do surely include making money, but that is usually rather low on their list of priorities. For this reason some of the measures of success applied to business ventures in general are not very useful or appropriate in measuring success in architecture. This is not to say that one should ignore good business practices; but one should recognize that there may be a perfectly valid reason for the architect to take some action that from a purely business-oriented view would not be good practice. The architect has different sources of potential gratification in his vocation from that of other businesspeople and to sublimate them would lead to personal dissatisfaction.

The other side of the coin is, of course, that someone who for compelling personal reasons feels that he must pursue a career in architecture may be one of life's most fortunate people. He is or will be in a field where, even when frustrations are high, the personal satisfactions can be thrilling and immense.

He will have the advantage of one of the best liberal-arts-education models available today, one that gives him a broader base than almost any other and in which the learning of the heart of the discipline, design, is by doing, not by memory. In the process of doing, he is discovering not only architecture but also himself and the architecture within himself. There is no right-and-only way to solve an architectural problem; there are only good, poor, and mediocre ways. In exploring and learning his way through the cumulative experiences of architectural-design studios, he is arming himself not with a store of memorized facts, but with a way of thinking, a way designed to help him get the most out of his potential creativity throughout his life.

Rejoice, young architect!

APPENDIX 1

Bibliography

GENERAL

American Institute of Architects. *Architect's Handbook of Professional Practice*. Looseleaf with periodically updated material, 2 vols. Washington, C.D.: AIA, 1973.

Coxe, Weld. *Managing Architectural and Engineering Practice*. New York: Wiley, 1980.

Dibner, David R. *Joint Ventures for Architects and Engineers*. New York: McGraw-Hill, 1972.

Foxhall, William B. *Professional Construction Management and Project Administration*. New York: AIA and McGraw-Hill, 1972.

——. *Techniques of Successful Practice for Architects and Engineers*. New York: McGraw-Hill, 1975.

Goleman, Harry A., ed. *Financial Real Estate Development*. Englewood, N.J.: AIA and Aloray, 1974.

Griffin, C. W. *Development Building, The Team Approach*. New York: AIA and Architectural Record, 1972.

Hunt, William Dudley, ed. *Comprehensive Architectural Services*. New York: AIA and McGraw-Hill, 1965.

Victor O. Shinnerer & Co., Inc. *Guidelines for Improved Practice*. Looseleaf series of papers issued periodically. Washington, D.C.: Shinnerer.

CODES

Hopf, Peter S. *Designer's Guide to OSHA*. New York: McGraw-Hill, 1975.

Sharry, John A., ed. *Life Safety Code Handbook*. Boston: National Fire Protection Association, 1978.

FINANCIAL

American Institute of Architects. *Compensation Management Guidelines for Architectural Services*. Washington, D.C.: AIA, 1975.

——. *The Economics of Architectural Practice*. Washington, D.C.: Case & Co., Inc., 1968.

———. *Profit Planning in Architectural Practice*. Washington, D.C.: Case &
Co., Inc., 1968.
Foote, Rosslyn F. *Running an Office for Fun and Profit*. Stroudsburg, PA:
Dowden, Hutchinson & Ross, 1978.

MARKETING

Coxe, Weld. *Marketing Architectural and Engineering Services*. New York:
Van Nostrand Reinhold, 1971.
Jones, Gerre. *How To Market Professional Design Services*. New York:
McGraw-Hill, 1973.
———. *How To Prepare Professional Design Brochures*. New York: McGraw-
Hill, 1976.
Kliment, Stephen A. *Creative Communications for a Successful Design Prac-
tice*. New York: Whitney, 1977.

PRODUCTION

Guidelines Publications. *Architectural Management*. Berkeley, CA:
Guidelines, 1969.
———. *Architectural Production*. Berkeley, CA: Guidelines, 1969.
———. *Breakthroughs in Architectural Practice*. Berkeley, CA: Guidelines,
1971.

TECHNICAL

Dell'Isola, Alphonse J. *Value Engineering in the Construction Industry*. New
York: Construction Publishing Co., 1973.
O'Brien, James J. *CPM in Construction Management*. New York: McGraw-
Hill, 1971.

APPENDIX 2

Typical Forms

GENERAL OFFICE MANAGEMENT FORMS:

A-1   TIME RECORD
A-2   LONG DISTANCE CALL RECORD

PROJECT MANAGEMENT FORMS:

B-1   PROJECT DATA FORM
B-2   GOVERNING CODES AND AGENCY REVIEW SCHEDULE
B-3   SHEET PLANNING FORM
B-4   CONTROL SHEET
     The cost and progress history of a project is
     summarized on this form.

BIDDING PHASE FORMS:

C-1   STATEMENT OF BIDDER'S QUALIFICATIONS
C-2   PLANS LOG
C-3   BID FORM (2 Sheets)
C-4   BID TABULATION

CONSTRUCTION ADMINISTRATION PHASE FORMS:

D-1   FIELD OBSERVATION REPORT FORM
D-2   SHOP DRAWING LOG
D-3   TRANSMITTAL LETTER
     This form can be used in any phase and for
     many purposes.
D-4   SPECIAL TRANSMITTAL LETTER
     Used for submittals on a specific project.

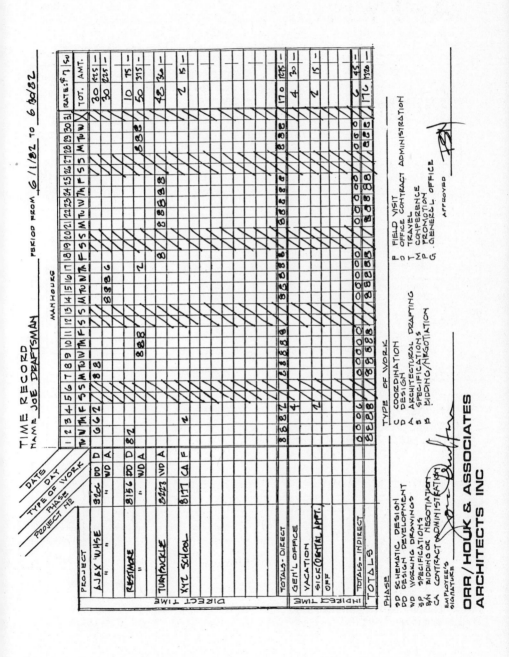

TIME RECORD
NAME JOE DRAFTSMAN
PERIOD FROM 6/1/82 TO 6/30/82

ORR/HOUK & ASSOCIATES
ARCHITECTS INC

A-1

LONG DISTANCE CALL RECORD

DATE	TIME	TO	TELEPHONE NO.	PROJECT NAME	NO.	REIMB YES	NO
6/23	1:10	SMITH, NEW YORK	212/555-0607	AJAX BARN	8232	X	
6/23	2:55	REV. JONES, MUDVILLE	555-2323	BUS. DEV/MT	—		X
6/24	9:33	GEO. ADAMS, CHICAGO	312/555-6677	OFFICE SUPPL.	—		X
6/25	10:15	SMITH, NEW YORK	212/555-0607	AJAX BARN	8232	X	
6/25	12:30	SAM BENNETT, LOS ANGELES	213/555-1879	KESTMORE	2156	X	

**ORR/HOUK & ASSOCIATES
ARCHITECTS INC**

A-2

<u>PROJECT DATA FORM</u>

DATE: **3/7/82**

PROJECT NAME : **RESTMORE RETIREMENT CENTER**

LOCATION: **CITY**

OWNER: **RESTMORE ASSOCIATES, INC.**

BUILDING TYPE : **APARTMENT**

PROGRAM : **120 - 160 APTS, 60% 1-BR, 30% 2-BR, 10%-
EFFIC. OR STUDIO, PARKING, DINING ROOM, KIT.,
CLINIC, HOBBY ROOMS, ETC. ADMIN. OFFICES.**

CONSTRUCTION BUDGET : $ **6,000,000**

COMPENSATION METHOD: **FIXED SUM**

CONSULTANTS:

STR'L: **WIDEFLANGE & ANCHORBOLT**
PHONE: **555- 6703**

HVAC: **MUCHO HOTAIRE, P.E.**
PHONE: **555- 3327**

PLBG: **PVC ENGINEERS**
PHONE: **555- 2812**

ELEC: **BRIGHT & DIM**
PHONE: **555- 5002**

OTHER: **FOOD SERVICE:
CHOWDOWN ASSOCS**
PHONE: **555- 6767**

PHONE:

DEADLINES:
COMPLETION & OCCUPANCY: **9/1/83**
OUT FOR BIDS: **8/15/82**
PRELIMINARIES: **5/31/82**
SCHEMATICS: **4/1/82**

REMARKS:

GOVERNING CODES AND AGENCY REVIEW SCHEDULE   F 59

PROJECT ACME OFFICE BLDG.

Project No. 8220

NOTE: Please initial and date each item when determined.

GOVERNING CODES AND ZONING

NFPA Yr._____   NBC Yr._____   Mechanical_____ Yr._____

SSBC Yr. 1979   State Code_____   Plumbing_____ Yr._____

UBC Yr._____   _____Yr._____   Electrical_____ Yr._____

BOCA Yr._____   Zoning CC ___Type   Fire District I __ Yr._____

BUILDING CLASSIFICATION: FIRE PROTECTION REQUIREMENTS: SELECTED U.L. DESIGN:

Occupancy Group BUSINESS   Columns____2____Hours   Columns # X301

Construction Type II ___ Beams_____2____Hours   Beams # Y716

Building Height 80 ____ft. Floors____2____Hours   Floors # G223

Front Yard 0 OR 20 ____ft. Roof_____1____Hours   Roof # P501

Side Yard____0_____ft. Partitions___1___Hours   Partitions # U404

Rear Yard____0_____ft. _____Hours   _____#_____

REVIEWING AGENCIES: (Check appropriate phase required for review by each agency.)

Agency	Name	Schematic	Design Dev.	Const. Doc.	Final Insp.
State Fire	F. MARSHALL	____		X	X
Local Fire	F. CHIEF	____	X	X	X
State Health	N/A	____			
Local Health	B. JOHN	____		X	X
Local Bldg. Insp.	B. PERMIT	____			X
Codes Admin.	N. ERNEST	X		X	
City Planning	N/A	____			
Environmental	N/A	____			
		____			

ARCHITECTS INC

B-2

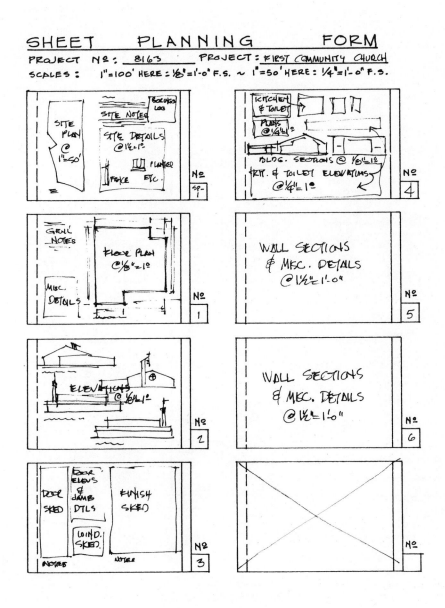

SHEET PLANNING FORM

PROJECT N°: 8163   PROJECT: FIRST COMMUNITY CHURCH

SCALES: 1"=100' HERE: 1/8"=1'-0" F.S. ~ 1"=50' HERE: 1/4"=1'-0" F.S.

CONTROL SHEET
CONTRACTOR: BUSHROD, INC.

PROJECT: ALLOWAY SCHOOL
PROJECT NO: 7823
DATE: 10/8/78

ITEMS	QUANTITY	OFFICE EST.	CONT. EST.	FINAL QUANTITY	FINAL COST	COST PER #	%TOT
GEN.CONTR,TAXES,INS.	—	105,000	(PROJECT B10)	—	121,600	6.24	16.79
SITEWORK-EXCAVATION	2070 CY	12,180		1850 CY	10,600	.51	1.38
CLEARING & GRADING	ALLOW.	2000		L.S.	2000	.10	.28
WALKS & PAVING	14,500 SY	26,500		15,000 SY	26,250	1.35	3.63
LANDSCAPING	ALLOW.	20,000		ALLOW.	20,000	1.03	2.76
CONCRETE-CAST IN PLACE	264	29,629		270	29,700	1.53	4.10
PRE CAST	—	—		—	—	—	—
MASONRY-BRICK	50,000	21,184		52,000	22,100	1.13	3.05
BLOCK	8000	15,370		8000	15,250	.78	2.11
METALS.-STRUCT.STEEL	27 T.	17,898		23.5 T.	16,575	.85	2.29
MISC. METALS	(IN STR'L STEEL)			2 T.	800	.04	.11
STL STUDS & DW	13,500 SF	17,700		13,750 SF	16,750	.86	2.31
CARPENTRY-ROUGH	L.S.	10,362		L.S.	12,500	.64	1.73
LAM, WOOD FINISHED	L.S.	16,126		L.S.	14,275	.73	1.97
WATERPROOFING	L.S	1022		L.S.	1500	.08	.21
WOOD DECK	12,694 SF	39,119		13,000 SF	39,000	2.00	5.39
INSULATION (IN ROOF'G)	—	—		—	—	—	—
ROOFING & SH. MTL	12,094 SF	8855		13,000 SF	7550	.38	1.04
SHEET METAL ROLL-UP GRILLE	1	2235		1	1875	.10	.26
METAL DOORS & FRAMES	12	6760		12	7500	.38	1.04
WOOD DOORS	48	9770		50	10,650	.52	1.39
WINDOWS	120	22,062		120	20,250	1.04	2.80
FINISHES-DRYWALL ON WD.	3500 SF	1155		3500 SF	1200	.06	.17
CER.TILE	3445 SF	10,335		3500 SF	9750	.50	1.35
CARPET RES.FLOORS	2200 SY	22,000		2350 SY	22,900	1.18	3.16
PAINTING	43,000 SF	7945		42,500 SF	8000	.41	1.11
WALL COVER'G	2095 SF	1628		2100 SF	1800	.09	.25
FINISH HARDWARE	L.S.	5700		L.S.	7500	.38	1.04
CABINETS	L.S.	15,000		L.S.	14,275	.73	1.91
CEILINGS	20,400 SF	9041		21,000 SF	10,075	.52	1.39
SPECIALTIES	L.S.	13,163		L.S.	12,000	.62	1.66
TOIL. PARTNS	8	1385		8	1250	.06	.17
MISC. KIT. EQUIP.	L.S.	27,500		ALLOW.	27,500	1.41	3.80
PLUMBING	L.S.	33,002		L.S.	32,000	1.64	4.42
MECHANICAL	L.S.	118,281		L.S.	115,375	5.92	15.94
ELECTRICAL	L.S.	73,764		L.S.	64,750	3.32	8.94
PROFIT (DISTRIBUTED)	—			—	—		
TOTAL	—	723,671		—	723,900	37.17	100.00

OVER / UNDER EST. #229 .03%

TOTAL AREA 19,475   19,475   SF @ $ 37.17

OVER / UNDER TIME(DAYS) 36 5%

REMARKS:

FILL IN MONTHS ——→ M A M J J A S O N D J F M

100%
80%
60%
40%
20%
0

B-4

STATEMENT OF BIDDER'S QUALIFICATIONS

Name of Bidder **WINNER CONSTRUCTION CO., INC.**

Business Address **222 WINNER'S CIRCLE, CITY**

When organized &/or incorporated **1970**

Number years doing business under present name **12**

Present Firm Name **SAME**

Financial or Bank reference **FIRST STATE BANK**

Address **FIRST STATE PLAZA, CITY**

Gross amount of Contracts in progress **$8,600,000**

Size and Character of organization

CORPORATE, 4 SUPT'S, OUR OWN FORCES

DO EARTHWORK, MASONRY & CONCRETE

Give three most recent jobs completed within price range of

this job and name of Architect

FIRST STATE BANK	**SMITH & SMITH**
MID-TOWN HOSPITAL ADD'N.	**JONES & JONES**
NORTHSIDE HIGH SCHOOL	**JONES & SMITH**

Have you ever refused to sign a contract at your original

bid? **NO**

Has a Bondsman of yours, while you were operating as an individual, partner, company or corporation ever been called on to
complete one of your jobs or indemnify the Owner? **NO**

Signed **B. A. Winner**

By **B. A. WINNER, PRES.**

PLANS LOG

PROJECT NUMBER __8106__

PROJECT NAME __AJAX WAREHOUSE__

SET NO.	TO	DEPOSIT	DATE	DATE RETURNED	DEPOSIT RETURNED
1	OWNER	—	2/6/82	—	—
2	OWNER	—	2/6/82	—	—
3	OFFICE SET	—	—	—	—
4	MP&E ENGINEERS	—	2/6/82	—	—
5	STR'L ENGINEERS	—	2/6/82	—	—
6	DODGE	—	2/6/82	—	—
7	DODGE (SCAN)	—	2/6/82	2/26/82	—
8	SMITH CONSTN CO	X	2/8/82	3/10/82	X
9	JONES CONSTN CO	X	2/7/82	3/12/82	X
10	DOE CONSTN CO	X	2/10/82	3/6/82	X
11	ROE CONSTN CO	X	2/9/82	2/12/82	X
12	WINNER CONSTN CO	X	2/10/82	—	X
13					
14					
15					
16					
17					
18					
19					
20					

B I D   F O R M - G E N E R A L

Gentlemen:

1. The undersigned has become familiar with the local
    conditions affecting the cost of the work and with the
    Drawings, General Conditions, Supplementary Conditions,
    General Requirements, and Specifications, and Standard
    Details, and all other applicable documents as indicated
    below:

    Bulletins numbered: *1, 2 & 3*

    all as prepared by

    ABC ARCHITECTS, INC.
    Nashville, TN

2. The undersigned hereby proposed to furnish all labor,
    materials, and equipment for the supplying and erection
    of the General Construction of

    First Community Church
    Nashville, Tennessee

    for a Base Bid of the sum of

    *SIX HUNDRED NINETY-THREE THOUSAND, SEVEN HUNDRED
    EIGHTY-TWO & NO/100* ——————Dollars ($ *693,782.00*)

    in accordance with the Contract Drawings and Specifications
    and other documents itemized in paragraph 1, above.

3. The undersigned estimates to complete the work for the
    Base Bid within   *240*   calendar days
    from the date of Notice to Proceed.

4. It is agreed that this Proposal may not be withdrawn for
    a period of forty-five (45) days from the date of the
    Proposal.

5. UNIT PRICES:

    Earth and/or Rock in excess of that predictable from
    data supplied in the Contract Documents:

      General Earth: $ 7$\frac{00}{}$ per yard

      General Rock: $ 17$\frac{00}{}$ per yard

      Trench Earth: $ 30$\frac{00}{}$ per yard

      Trench Rock: $ 75$\frac{00}{}$ per yard

6. ALTERNATIVES: ADD

      Alternate No. 1, add the tower $ 44,000.00

      Alternate No. 2, add the skylights   3,000.00

FIRM NAME   GAPE, INC

BY (signature)   George M. Gape

TITLE   PRESIDENT

DATE   10/19/82

C-3 (cont.)

BID TABULATIONS
FIRST COMMUNITY CHURCH · 2PM · 10/19/82   ABC ARCHITECTS, INC.

CONTRACTOR	# BULLETINS 2 1 1 2 3					ADDO	SARS	BASE BID	CAL. DAYS	UNIT PRICES				ALTERNATES	
										GENERAL EARTH	GENERAL ROCK	TRENCH EARTH	TRENCH ROCK	1	2
DANDY, CONSTN CO.	X	X	X	X	X	X	1	856,196	300	4.00	23.00	20.00	100.00	63,340	7,000
J.R. FARRELL	X	X	X	X	X	X	1	707,740	240	9.00	15.00	11.00	70.00	59,998	3,818
GAPE, INC.	X	X	X	X	X	X	X	693,782	240	7.00	17.00	30.00	75.00	44,000	3,000
REGAL, CONSTN CO.	X	X	X	X	X	X	X	715,800	270	—	—	—	—	55,000	5,200
SAGE & THYME	X	X	X	X	X	X	1	794,500	210	10.00	46.00	15.00	50.00	56,000	4,900
WINDSOR CONSTN CO.	X	X	X	X	X	X	X	787,000	240	4.00	20.00	16.00	48.00	58,000	6,000

C-4

TO: GEORGE MICHAELS

PROJECT: MICHAELS, INC. OFFICE BLDG.
DATE OF VISIT: 5/8/82
TIME: 10 AM
WEATHER: SUNNY, 72°
PRESENT AT SITE: ARCHT., MECH. ENGINEER, PROJ. SUPT.

GENERAL:

INSPECTED GENERAL CONSTN. WORK IS
APPROX. 3 WKS BEHIND SKED. DOOR Nº 38
IS WARPED & WILL HAVE TO BE REPLACED.
BRICK HAS NOT BEEN PROPERLY CLEANED.
MECH. ENGINEER WILL SUBMIT SEPARATE
REPORT.

COPIES TO: MECH. ENGINEER, CONTRACTOR

SUBMITTED BY: [signature]

FIELD OBSERVATION

SHOP DRAWING LOG

JOB: TURN BUCKLE SUPERMARKET   JOB. No. 8162   CONTR. HARDHAT, INC.

No.	DESCRIPTION	DATE RECV'D	TO CONSULTANT	REC'VD FROM CONSULTANT	RET'D TO CONTR.	ACTION TAKEN
1	PROG. SKED	4/6/82	—	—	4/10/82	APP. AS NOTED
2	REINF. STEEL	4/8/82	4/8/82	4/19/82	4/20/82	APP.
3	CONC. DESIGN MIX	4/8/82	4/8/82	4/19/82	4/20/82	APP.
4	DAMPPROOFING	4/15/82	—	—	4/30/82	APP.
5	HOLLOWMETAL	4/15/82	—	—	4/30/82	APP. AS NOTED
6	STR'L & MISC. STEEL	4/30/82	4/30/82	5/12/82	5/14/82	APP.
7	STOREFRONT	4/30/82	—	—	5/14/82	APP.
8	FINISH HARDWARE	5/6/82	—	—	5/20/82	APP. AS NOTED
9	ELEC. LIGHT FIXT. & GEAR	5/16/82	5/16/82	5/27/82	5/27/82	APP. AS NOTED
10	MECHANICAL EQUIP	5/16/82	5/16/82	6/6/82	6/6/82	APP. AS NOTED
11	PLUMBING FIXTS.	5/16/82	5/16/82	6/6/82	6/6/82	APP.
12	MILLWORK	5/20/82	—	—	6/10/82	REJECT-RESUB.
13	REFRIG. CASEWORK	6/6/82	6/6/82	6/12/82	6/17/82	APP.
14	FIXTURES	6/6/82	6/6/82	—	6/18/82	APP.
15	SIGNS	7/16/82	7/16/82	7/23/82	7/23/82	APP. AS NOTED
12A	MILLWORK RESUBMITTAL	7/20/82	—	—	7/30/82	APP.

TRANSMITTAL LETTER

TO: ~~BOB~~ WINNER   PROJECT: MUNICIPAL OFFICE BLDG.

WINNER CONSTN CO. INC.

222 WINNER'S CIRCLE   PROJECT NO: 8146

CITY   DATE: 6/12/82

WE ARE SENDING YOU THE FOLLOWING:

COPIES	DESCRIPTION	AS REQUESTED	SEE REMARKS	APPROVED	APPROVED AS NOTED	RESUBMIT	REJECTED
4	HOLLOW METAL SUBMITTAL				X		

REMARKS: _____

_____

_____

_____

COPY TO: _____   BY: _____

ARCHITECTS INC

transmittal letter
keep original letter with submittal package

(5)

contractor: GUYBOLT ENGINEERS

architect: FRANK ORR / CAIN · SCHLOTT

JOE L EVINS
APPALACHIAN CENTER for CRAFTS
DEKALB COUNTY TENNESSEE
SBC No. 529 / 80-01-76

ADMINISTRATION BUILDING
PHASE II

→ OHMSMORE ELECTRIC COMPANY

ITEM _____ Electrical Fixtures

NUMBER 16010
use specs section no for submittal

RECEIVED DATE	BY	ACTION	BY	TO	COPIES	DATE
12-17-77 Guybolt		Approved	Ralph Martin	Frank Orr	8	12-19-77
12/22/77	to	TRANSMITTED	to	ANDERSON & ASSOCS.	8	12/24/77
1/31/78	KSA	TRANSMITTED *	ANDERSON & ASSOS	FRANK ORR	6	1/31/78
1/31/78	to	TRANSMITTED	to	RALPH MARTIN	5	1/31/78

NOTES: * SEE ANDERSON'S STAMP IN SUBMITTAL -
PANELS HB & LB & FIXTURE C : APPROVED AS NOTED.
FIXTURE TYPES B, D, L & M: REJECTED, RESUBMIT
ALL OTHERS APPROVED.

Index

accounting, 66–67, 72–73; *see also* bookkeeping
administration, 50
agreement, standard: *see* American Institute of Architects; contracts
AIA: *see* American Institute of Architects
air conditioning, 28, 31, 108; *see also* engineers, mechanical
American Institute of Architects (AIA)
  documents, 28, 42–43, 51, 86–87, 93
  publications, 76–77, 78
  standard agreement, 13, 28, 42–43, 51, 86–87, 93
architect
  as businessperson, 5–7, 12, 74–77, 123–25
  and clients, 13–16, 86–88
  and constructors, 11, 22–27
  and consultants, 28, 32–33
  and engineers, 28, 32–33, 98–99
  and ethics, 20–21, 25–27
  and government, 11, 34–40, 120
  image of, 17
  liabilities, legal, 40, 61–62, 73
  responsibilities, 18–20, 21, 25, 32, 95, 99
  see also designer
architect's seal, 62
architectural drawings, 88, 90–92, 94
architecture
  as art, 21
  landscape, 17, 116
arms-length relationships, 25
associate, 63; *see also* partnership

banks, 10
base bid, 101–102
bid bond, 100
bid deposits, 104–105
bidding, 100–104
bid documents, 100–101
billing, 66–67, 75
billing rate, 66–67, 75
BOCA: see Building Officials
    Code Authority
bonds
    bid, 100
    performance, 23
bookkeeping, 72–73; see also
    accounting
Breuer, Marcel, 20
brokers, 10
budget, 86–87; see also finances
building codes, 36, 41–43,
    93–94
Building Officials Code Author-
    ity (BOCA), 36
building permit, 11, 37
business practices: see finances;
    management; organization

capital, 78
cash flow, 6, 71–72; see also
    revenue
catalogs, manufacturers', 96
certificate of need, 39
church, as client, 15
civil engineering, 33
clients, 13–16, 86–88; nonpro-
    fit, 15; see also owner
codes, building, 36, 41–43,
    93–94
codes, fire, 36
compensation, methods of,
    74–77
    direct multiple, 75
    fixed sum, 76

percentage, 75
professional fee, 75–76
computerization, 67–68, 121
conflict of interest, 25; see also
    ethics
construction
    costs, 75
    documents, 92, 94–99
    industry, 3–6, 8–9
    process, 8–9, 22–27
constructors, 11, 22–27
consultants, 28–33
consumers, 12–13; see also
    clients
contractors: see constructors
contracts
    administration, 52–53,
        105–10
    AIA standard, 13, 28, 42–43,
        51, 86–87, 93
    specifications, 43
copyright, 99
corporation, 61–63; small busi-
    ness, 61
cost plus, 74, 75
Coxe, Weld, 118–19
Creighton, Wilbur, 26

data processing, 67–68
delivery, product, 119–20
design
    development, 91, 93–94
    interior, 113–14
    schematic, 89–90
design-build, 26–27, 119
designer, 11, 14–15; see also
    architect
design office
    division of labor, 47–48
    management, 50–51, 64–70,
        80–85
    organization, 55–58

personnel, 64–66
space, 69–70, 117–19
developer, 5, 8–9, 10, 13
documents, 92, 94–99; AIA,
    101, 106
Dodge, F.W., Corporation, 101
drawings, architectural, 88,
    90–92, 94
    as communication, 88
    shop, 108–109

economy, U.S., 3–4, 6–7; see
    also capital
education, professional, 121–22
educational facilities, 39
electrical engineer, 31–32
employees, 64–66; see also
    consultants
energy, 112–13, 120–21
engineering, 18–20, 29–32,
    98–99
engineers
    electrical, 31–32
    mechanical, 30–31, 108
    structural, 29–30, 98–99
environmental protection agen-
    cies, 39
equity, 11
estimates, 89, 93
ethics, professional, 20–21,
    26–27; see also conflict of
    interest

fast tracking, 119–20
feasibility studies, 20, 113
fees, 74, 75–76; see also com-
    pensation
filing, 65, 81–83; storage, 83–84
finances, 5–6, 10–11, 71–79
    management of, 71–79
    planning, 77–79

see also budget; compensa-
    tion; revenue
fire code, 36
fixed sum, 74, 76–77
furniture design, 20

government
    jurisdiction, 34
    project initiator, 5, 8
    regulations, 11, 34–40,
        93–94, 120
    see also codes; zoning
guarantees, contractual, 53

handicapped, accessibility for,
    5, 39
health, public, 5, 7
health-care facilities, 39
heating, 28, 31, 108; see also
    engineers, mechanical
horizontal organization, 55–56,
    58
housing, 35
HVAC (heating, ventilation, air
    conditioning), 28, 31, 108;
    see also engineers,
    mechanical

income: see compensation
incorporation, 61–63; small
    business, 61
inspections, 52–53, 106
insurance, liability, 94
insurance companies, 10
interest rate, 10
interior design, 113–14
investment, 5–6, 10

joint venture, 20, 24

landscape architecture, 17, 116
laws: see codes; government;
    regulation; zoning

lawyers, 73
liability, professional, 40,
    61–62, 73; insurance, 94
licenses, 23
liquidation, 53
litigation, 73
logs, manhour, 96–98
lump sum, 74, 76–77

management, business, 7, 12;
    see also finances; or-
    ganization
management, financial, 71–79
management, office, 64–70,
    80–85
manhours, 96–98
marketing, 48–50, 68–69
master planning, 114–16
mechanical engineer, 30–31,
    108; see also HVAC
microfilm, 83–84
mortgage, 10
mortgage banker, 10
multiplier, 66–67

Nashville (Tennessee) State
    Capitol, 26
National Council of Architec-
    tural Registration Boards
    NCARB), 121–22
National Fire Protective Asso-
    ciation (NFPA), 36
NCARB: see National Council of
    Architectural Registration
    Boards
negotiation, 100, 103–104; see
    also bidding
NFPA: see National Fire Pro-
    tective Association
nonprofit organization, 15, 39
notebook, project, 82–83

Occupational Safety and Health
    Act (OSHA), 39–40
office, design
    division of labor, 47–48
    management, 50–51, 64–70,
        80–85
    organization, 55–58
    personnel, 64–66
    space, 69–70, 117–19
ordinances, zoning, 11, 35,
    41–43
organization
    horizontal, 55–56, 58
    vertical, 55, 57–58
OSHA: see Occupational Safety
    and Health Act
owner, 12, 13–14; see also
    clients
ownership, 59–63; see also cor-
    poration; partnership; sole
    proprietorship

partners, 58–59
partnership, 58–59, 60–61
payments, 106
performance bond, 23
permit, building, 11, 37
personnel, 64–66; see also
    consultants
planned unit development
    (PUD), 35–36
planning, 114–16
plumbing, 30; see also HVAC
Portman, John, 15
printing costs, 104–105
production, 51–52
profit motive, 8, 78–79
program, 87–88
progress, schedule of, 106–108
project
    closeout, 53, 110–11
    management, 80–85

manual, 43, 98
notebook, 82–83
  see also office, design
public interest, 5, 7, 13
PUD: see planned unit development
punch list, 110

real estate, 113
registration, 121–22
regulation, 11, 34–40, 93–94, 120; see also codes; government; zoning
retainage, 111
revenue, 73–77
  collection, 73–75
  compensation, 74–77
  see also finances

safety, public, 5, 7, 34–35, 39
salary: see compensation
samples, 108
savings-and-loan associations, 10
schedules, 53, 106–108
schematic designs, 89–90
seal, architect's, 62
shop drawings, 108–109
small business corporation, 61
sole proprietorship, 59–60, 78, 84

specifications, 43
staff: see personnel
Standard Building Code, 36
storage methods, 83–84
Strickland, William, 26
structural engineer, 29–30, 98–99
submittals, 108–110
supervision, 52
Sweets' catalogs, 96

tax laws, 62, 66, 120
Tennessee State Capitol, 26

Uniform Buildings Code, 36
urban design, 116

variance, zoning, 37
ventilation, 28, 31, 108; see also engineers, mechanical
vertical organization, 55, 57–58

warranty: see guarantee
word processor, 67
work-flow diagram, 95

zoning, 11, 34–38, 41–43
  ordinances, 11, 35, 41–43
  variance, 37